M
INDIA

Edward James 'Jim' Corbett (25 July 1875–19 April 1955) was an Anglo-Indian hunter and tracker-turned-conservationist, author and naturalist, famous for hunting a large number of man-eating tigers and leopards in India. He played a key role in creating a national reserve for the endangered Bengal tiger in what is now Uttarakhand. In 1957, the national park was renamed Jim Corbett National Park in his honour.

MY INDIA

JIM CORBETT

RUPA

Published by
Rupa Publications India Pvt. Ltd 2018
7/16, Ansari Road, Daryaganj
New Delhi 110002

Sales centres:
Bengaluru Chennai
Hyderabad Jaipur Kathmandu
Kolkata Mumbai Prayagraj

P-ISBN: 978-93-5304-066-6
E-ISBN: 978-93-5304-067-3

Thirteenth impression 2024

15 14 13

Printed in India

If you are looking for a history of India, or for an account of the rise and fall of the British raj, or for the reason for the cleaving of the subcontinent into two mutually antagonistic parts and the effect this mutilation will have on the respective sections, and ultimately on Asia, you will not find it in these pages; for though I have spent a lifetime in the country, I lived too near the seat of events, and was too intimately associated with the actors, to get the perspective needed for the impartial recording of these matters.

In my India—the India I know—there are four hundred million people, 90 per cent of whom are simple, honest, brave, loyal, hard-working souls whose daily prayer to God, and to whatever Government is in power, is to give them security of life and of property to enable them to enjoy the fruits of their labours. It is of these people, who are admittedly poor, and who are often described as 'India's starving millions', among whom I have lived and whom I love, that I shall endeavor to tell in the pages of this book, which I humbly dedicate to my friends, the poor of India.

Contents

Introduction

Having read my dedication you may ask: 'Who are these poor of India that you mention?' 'What do you mean by "my India"?' The questions are justified. The world has developed the habit of using the word 'Indian' to denote an inhabitant of the great peninsula that stretches upwards of two thousand miles from north to south, and as much from east to west. Geographically the term may pass muster, but when it comes to applying it to the people themselves, one should not, without further explanation, use a description whose looseness has already led to infinite misunderstanding. The four hundred million people of India are divided horizontally by race, tribe and caste into a far greater diversity than exists in Europe, and they are cleft vertically by religious differences fully as deep as those which sunder any one nation from another. It was religion, not race, that split the Indian Empire into Hindustan and Pakistan.

Let me, therefore, explain what I mean by the title of this book.

'My India', about which these sketches of village life and work are written, refers to those portions of a vast land which I have known from my earliest days, and where I have worked, and the simple folk whose ways and characters I have tried to depict for you are those among whom I spent the greater part of seventy years. Look at a map of India. Pick out Cape Comorin, the most southerly point of the peninsula, and run your eye straight up to where the Gangetic Plain slopes up into the foothills of the Himalayas in the north of the United Provinces. There you will find the hill station of Nainital, the summer seat of the Government of the United Provinces, packed from April to November with Europeans and wealthier Indians seeking escape from the heat of the plains, and occupied during the winter only by a few permanent residents, of whom most of my life I was one. Now leave this hill station and run your eye down the Ganges River on its way to the sea, past Allahabad, Benares, and Patna, till you reach Mokameh Ghat, where I laboured for twenty-one years. The scenes of my sketches centre round these two points in India: Nainital and Mokameh Ghat.

In addition to many footpaths, Nainital is accessible by a motor road of which we are justly proud, for it has the reputation of being the best-aligned and the best-maintained hill road in India. Starting at the railway terminus of Kathgodam, the road, in its course of twenty-two miles, passes through forests where occasionally the tiger and the dreaded hamadryad can be seen, and climbs 4,500 feet by easy gradients to Nainital. The place can best be described as an open valley running east and west, surrounded on three sides by hills, the highest of which, Cheena, rises to a height of 8,569 feet.

It is open at the end from which the motor road approaches it. Nestling in the valley is a lake a little more than two miles in circumference, fed at the upper end by a perennial spring and overflowing at the other end where the motor road terminates. At the upper and lower ends of the valley there are bazaars, and the surrounding wooded hills are dotted with residential houses, churches, schools, clubs and hotels. Near the margin of the lake are boat houses, a picturesque Hindu temple, and a very sacred rock shrine presided over by an old Brahmin priest who has been a lifelong friend of mine.

Geologists differ in their opinion as to the origin of the lake, some attributing it to glaciers and landslides, others to volcanic action. Hindu legends, however, give the credit for the lake to three ancient sages, Atri, Pulastya and Pulaha. The sacred book Skanda Purana tells how, while on a penitential pilgrimage, these three sages arrived at the crest of Cheena and, finding no water to quench their thirst, dug a hole at the foot of the hill and syphoned water into it from Manasarovar, the sacred lake in Tibet. After the departure of the sages the goddess Naini arrived and took up her abode in the waters of the lake. In course of time forests grew on the sides of the excavation and, attracted by the water and the vegetation, birds and animals in great numbers made their home in the valley. Within a radius of four miles of the goddess' temple I have, in addition to other animals, seen a tiger, leopard, bear and sambhar, and in the same area identified 128 varieties of birds. Rumours of the existence of the lake reached the early administrators of this part of India, and as the hill people were unwilling to disclose the position of their sacred lake, one of these administrators, in the year 1839, hit on the ingenious plan of placing a large stone on the head of a hill man, telling him he would have to carry it until he arrived at goddess Naini's lake. After wandering over the hills for many days, the man eventually got tired of carrying the stone, and led the party who were following him, to the lake. The stone alleged to have been carried by the man was shown to me when I was a small boy, and when I remarked that it was a very big stone for a man to carry—it weighed about six hundred pounds—the hill man who showed it to me said, 'Yes, it is a big stone, but you must remember that in those days our people were very strong'.

Provide yourself now with a good pair of field glasses and accompany me to the top of Cheena. From here you will get a bird's-eye view of the country surrounding Nainital. The road is steep, but if you are interested in birds, trees and flowers, you will not mind the three-mile climb and if you arrive at the top thirsty, as the three sages did, I will show you a crystal-clear spring of cold water to quench your thirst. Having rested and eaten your lunch, turn now to the north. Immediately below you is a deep, well-wooded valley running down to the Kosi River. Beyond the river are a number of parallel ridges with villages dotted here and there; on one of these ridges is the town of Almora, and on another, the cantonment of Ranikhet. Beyond these again are more ridges, the highest of which, Dungar Buqual, rises to a height of 14,200 feet and is dwarfed into insignificance by the mighty mass of the snow-clad Himalayas.

Sixty miles due north of you, as the crow flies, is Trisul, and to the east and to the west of this imposing 23,406-foot peak, the snow mountains stretch in an unbroken line for many hundreds of miles. Where the snow fades out of sight, to the west of Trisul are first of the Gangotri group, then the glaciers and mountains above the sacred shrines of Kedarnath and Badrinath, and then Kamet made famous by mountaineer Frank Smythe.

To the east of Trisul, and set farther back, you can just see the top of Nanda Devi (25,689 feet), one of the highest mountains in India. To your right front is Nanda Kot, the spotless pillow of the goddess Parvati, and a little farther east are the beautiful peaks of Panchchuli, the 'five cooking-places' used by the Pandavas while on their way to Kailash in Tibet. At the first approach of dawn, while Cheena and the intervening hills are still shrouded in the mantle of night, the snowy range changes from indigo blue to rose pink, and as the sun touches the peaks nearest to heaven, the pink gradually changes to dazzling white. During the day the mountains show up cold and white, each crest trailing a feather of powdered snow, and in the setting sun the scene may be painted pink, gold, or red according to the fancy of heaven's artist.

Turn your back now on the snow and face south. At the limit of your range of vision you will see three cities: Bareilly, Kashipur and Moradabad. These three cities, the nearest of which, Kashipur, is some fifty miles as the crow flies, are on the main railway that runs between Calcutta and Punjab. There are three belts of country between the railway and the foothills: first, a cultivated belt some twenty miles wide, then a grass belt ten miles wide known as the Terai, and third, a tree belt ten miles wide known as the Bhabar. In the Bhabar belt, which extends right up to the foothills, clearings have been made, and on this rich fertile soil, watered by many streams, villages of varying sizes have been established. The nearest group of villages, Kaladhungi, is fifteen miles from Nainital by road, and at the upper end of this group you will see our village, Choti Haldwani, surrounded by a three-mile- long stone wall. Only the roof of our cottage, which is at the junction of the road running down from Nainital with the road skirting the foothills, is visible in a group of big trees. The foothills in this area are composed almost entirely of iron ore, and it was at Kaladhungi that iron was first smelted in northern India. The fuel used was wood, and as the 'King of Kumaon', General Sir Henry Ramsay, feared that the furnaces would consume all the forests in the Bhabar, he closed down the foundries. Between

Kaladhungi and your seat on Cheena the low hills are densely wooded with sal, the trees which supply our railways with ties, or sleepers, and in the nearest fold of the ridge nestles the little lake of Khurpatal, surrounded by fields on which the best potatoes in India are grown.

Away in the distance, to the right, you can see the sun glinting on the Ganges, and to the left you can see it glinting on the Sarda; the distance between these two rivers where they leave the foot hills is roughly two hundred miles.

Now turn to the east and before you, in the near and middle distance, you will see the country described in old gazetteers as 'the district of sixty lakes'. Many of these lakes have silted up, some in my lifetime and the only ones of any size that now remain are Naini Tal, Sat Tal, Bhim Tal and Naukuchia Tal. Beyond Naukuchia Tal is the cone-shaped hill, Choti Kailash. The gods do not favour the killing of bird or beast on this sacred hill, and the last man who disregarded their wishes—a soldier on leave during the war—unaccountably lost his footing, after killing a mountain goat and, in full view of his two companions, fell a thousand feet into the valley below.

Beyond Choti Kailash is the Kala Agar ridge on which I hunted the Chowgarh man-eating tiger for two years, and beyond this ridge, the mountains of Nepal fade out of sight. Turn now to the west. But first it will be necessary for you to descend a few hundred feet and take up a new position on Deopatta, a rocky peak 7,991 feet high, adjoining Cheena. Immediately below you is a deep, wide and densely wooded valley which starts on the saddle between Cheena and Deopatta and extends through Dachouri to Kaladhungi. It is richer in flora and fauna than any other in the Himalayas, and beyond this beautiful valley the hills extend in an unbroken line up to the Ganges, the waters of which you can see glinting in the sun over a hundred miles away. On the far side of the Ganges are the Siwalik range of hills—hills that were old before the mighty Himalayas were born.

1

The Queen of the Village

Come with me now to one of the villages you saw in your bird's-eye view from the top of Cheena. The parallel lines you saw etched across the face of the hill are terraced fields. Some of these are no more than ten feet wide, and the stone walls supporting them are in some cases thirty feet high. The ploughing of these narrow fields, with a steep hill on one side and a big drop on the other, is a difficult and a dangerous job, and is only made possible by the use of a plough with a short shaft and of cattle that have been bred on the hills and that are in consequence, small and stocky, and as sure-footed as goats. The stout-hearted people, who, with infinite labour, have made these terraced fields, live in a row of stone houses with slate roofs bordering the rough and narrow road that runs from the Bhabar and the plains beyond, to the inner Himalayas. The people in this village know me, for in response to an urgent telegram, which the whole village subscribed to send me, and which was carried by runner to Nainital for transmission, I once came hot-foot from Mokameh Ghat, where I was working, to rid them of a man- eating tiger.

The incident which necessitated the sending of the telegram took place at midday in a field just above the row of houses. A woman and her twelve-year-old daughter were reaping wheat when a tiger suddenly appeared. As the girl attempted to run to her mother for protection, the tiger struck at her, severed her head from her body, and catching the body in mid-air, bounded away into the jungle adjoining the field, leaving the head near the mother's feet. Telegrams, even urgent ones, take long in transmission, and as I had to do a journey of a thousand miles by rail and road, and the last twenty miles on foot, a week elapsed between the sending of the telegram and my arrival at the village; and in the meantime, the tiger made another kill.

The victim on this occasion was a woman who, with her husband and children, had lived for years in the compound of the house adjoining our home in Nainital. This woman, in company with several others, was cutting grass on the hill above the village when she was attacked by the tiger, killed, and carried off in full view of her companions. The screams of the frightened women were heard in the village, and, while the women were running back to Nainital to report the tragedy, the men of the village assembled and with great gallantry drove away the tiger. Knowing—with an Indian's trust—that I would respond to the telegram they had sent me, they wrapped the body in a blanket and tied it to the topmost branch of a thirty-foot rhododendron tree. From the tiger's subsequent actions it was evident that he had been lying up close by and had watched these proceedings, for if he had not seen the body being put up in a tree, he would never have found it, as tigers have no sense of smell.

When the women made their report in Nainital, the husband of the dead woman came to my sister Maggie and told her of the killing of his wife, and at crack of dawn next morning Maggie sent out some of our men to make a machan over the kill and to sit on the machan until I came, for I was expected to arrive that day. Materials for making the machan were procured at the village and, accompanied by the villagers, my men proceeded to the rhododendron tree, where it was found that the tiger had climbed the tree, torn a hole in the blanket, and carried away the body. Again with commendable courage—for they were unarmed—the villagers and my men followed up the drag for half a mile; and on finding the partly eaten body, they started to put up a machan in an oak tree immediately above it. Just as the machan was completed, a sportsman from Nainital, who was out on an all-day shoot, arrived quite by accident at the spot and, saying he was a friend of mine, he told my men to go away, as he would sit up for the tiger himself. So, while my men returned to Nainital to make their report to me— for I had arrived in the meantime— the sportsman, his gun bearer and a man carrying his lunch basket and a lantern, took up their positions on the machan.

There was no moon, and an hour after dark, the gun-bearer asked the sportsman why he had allowed the tiger to carry away the kill, without firing at it. Refusing to believe that the tiger had been anywhere near the kill, the sportsman lit the lantern, and as he was letting it down, on a length of string, to illuminate the ground, the string slipped through his fingers and the lantern crashed to the ground and caught fire. It was the month of May, when our forests are very dry, and within a minute, the dead grass and brushwood at the foot of the tree were burning fiercely. With great courage, the sportsman shinned down the tree and attempted to beat out the flames with his tweed coat, until he suddenly remembered the man- eater and hurriedly climbed back to the machan. He left his coat, which was on fire, behind him.

The illumination from the fire revealed the fact that the kill was indeed gone, but the sportsman at this stage had lost all interest in kills and his anxiety now was for his own safety, and for the damage the fire would do to the Government forest. Fanned by a strong wind, the fire receded from the vicinity of the tree and eight hours later a heavy downpour of rain and hail extinguished it, but not before it had burnt out several square miles of forest. It was the sportsman's first attempt to make contact with a man-eater and, after his experience of first nearly having been roasted and later having been frozen, it was also his last. Next morning, while he was making his weary way back to Nainital by one road, I was on my way out to the village by another, in ignorance of what had happened the previous night.

At my request, the villagers took me to the rhododendron tree and I was amazed to see how determined the tiger had been to regain possession of his kill. The torn blanket was some twenty-five feet from the ground, and the claw marks on the tree, the condition of the soft ground and the broken brushwood at the foot of it, showed that the tiger had climbed and fallen off the tree at least twenty times before he eventually succeeded in tearing a hole in die blanket and removing the body.

From this spot, the tiger had carried the body half a mile, to the tree on which the machan had been built. Beyond this point the fire had obliterated all trace of a drag but, following on the line I thought the tiger would have taken, a mile farther on, I stumbled on the charred head of the woman. A hundred yards beyond this spot there was heavy cover which the fire had not reached and for hours I searched this cover, right down to the foot of the valley five miles away, without, however, finding any trace of the tiger.

Five people lost their lives between the accidental arrivals of the sportsman at the machan, and the shooting of the tiger. I arrived back in the village, after my fruitless search of the cover, late in the evening, and the wife of the headman prepared for me a meal which her daughters placed before me on brass plates. After a very generous, and a very welcome meal—for I had eaten nothing that day—I picked up the plates with the intention of washing them in a nearby spring. Seeing my intention, the three girls ran forward and relieved me of the plates, saying, with a toss of their heads and a laugh, that it would not break their caste—they were Brahmins—to wash the plates from which the White Sadhu had eaten.

The headman is dead now and his daughters have married and left the village, but his wife is alive, and you, who are accompanying me to the village, after your bird's-eye view from Cheena, must be prepared to drink the tea, not made with water but with rich, fresh milk sweetened with jaggery, which she will brew for us. Our approach down the steep hillside facing the village has been observed and a small square of frayed carpet and two wicker chairs, reinforced with ghooral skins, have been set ready for us. Standing near these chairs to welcome us is the wife of the headman; there is no purdah here and she will not be embarrassed if you take a good look at her, and she is worth looking at. Her hair, snow-white now, was raven-black when I first knew her, and her cheeks, which in those far-off days had a bloom on them, are now ivory-white, without a single crease or wrinkle. Daughter of a hundred generations of Brahmins, her blood is as pure as that of the ancestor who founded her line.

Pride of pure ancestry is inherent in all men, but nowhere

is there greater respect for pure ancestry than there is in India. There are several different castes of people in the village this dear old lady administers, but her rule is never questioned and her word is law, not because of the strong arm of retainers, for of these she has none, but because she is a Brahmin, the salt of India's earth.

The high prices paid in recent years for field produce have brought prosperity—as it is known in India—to this hill village, and of this prosperity, our hostess has had her full share. The string of fluted gold beads that she brought as part of her dowry are still round her neck, but the thin silver necklace has been deposited in the family bank, the hole in the ground under the cooking-place, and her neck is now encircled by a solid gold band. In the far-off days her ears were unadorned, but now she has number of thin gold rings in the upper cartilage, and from her nose hangs a gold ring five inches in diameter, the weight of which is partly carried by a thin gold chain looped over her right ear. Her dress is the same as that worn by all high-caste hill women: a shawl, a tight-fitting bodice of warm material, and a voluminous sprint skirt. Her feet are bare, for even in these advanced days the wearing of shoes among our hill folk denotes that the wearer is unchaste.

The old lady has now retired to the inner recesses of her house to prepare tea, and while she is engaged on this pleasant task you can turn your attention to the bania's shop on the other side of the narrow road. The bania, too, is an old friend. Having greeted us and presented us with a packet of cigarettes he has gone back to squat cross-legged on the wooden platform on which his wares are exposed. These wares consist of the few articles that the village folk and wayfarers need in the way of atta, rice, dal, ghee, salt, stale sweets purchased at a discount in the Nainital bazaar, hill potatoes fit for the table of a king, enormous turnips so fierce that when eaten in public they make the onlookers' eyes water, cigarettes and matches, a tin of kerosene oil, and near the platform and within reach of his hand, an iron pan in which milk is kept simmering throughout the day.

As the bania takes his seat on the platform, his few customers gather in front of him. First is a small boy, accompanied by an even smaller sister, who is the proud possessor of one pice, all of which he is anxious to invest in sweets. Taking the pice from the small grubby hand, the bania drops it into an open box. Then, waving his hand over the tray to drive away the wasps and flies, he picks up a square sweet made of sugar and curd, breaks it in half and puts a piece into each eager outstretched hand.

Next comes a woman of the depressed class who has two annas to spend on her shopping. One anna is invested in atta, the coarse ground wheat that is the staple food of our hill folk, and two pice in the coarsest of the three qualities of dal exposed on the stall. With the remaining two pice she purchases a little salt and one of the fierce turnips and then, with a respectful salaam to the bania, for he is a man who commands respect, she hurries off to prepare the midday meal for her family.

While the woman is being served, the shrill whistles and shouts of men herald the approach of a string of pack mules, carrying cloth from the Moradabad handlooms to the markets in the interior of the hills. The sweating mules have had a stiff climb up the rough road from the foothills. A pice is worth about a farthing, but is itself made up of three smaller coins called pies. Four pice make an anna, sixteen annas a rupee and while they are having a breather, the four men in charge have sat down on the bench provided by the bania for his customers and are treating themselves to a cigarette and a glass of milk. Milk is the strongest drink that has ever been served at this shop, or at any other of the hundreds of wayside shops throughout the hills, for, except for those few who have come in contact with what is called civilization, our hill men do not drink.

Drinking among women, in my India, is unknown. No daily paper has ever found its way into this village, and the only news the inhabitants get of the outside world is from an occasional trip into Nainital and from wayfarers, the best-informed of whom are the packmen. On their way into the hills they bring news of the distant plains of India, and on their return journey a month or so later, they have news from the trading centers where they sell their wares.

The tea the old lady has prepared for us is now ready. You must be careful how you handle the metal cup filled to the brim, for it is hot enough to take the skin off your hands. Interest has now shifted from the packmen to us, and whether or not you like the sweet, hot liquid, you must drink every drop of it, for the eyes of the entire village, whose guest you are, are on you, and to leave any dregs in your cup would mean that you did not consider the drink good enough for you.

Others have attempted to offer recompense for hospitality but we will not make this mistake, for these simple and hospitable people are intensely proud, and it would be as great an insult to offer to pay the dear old lady for her cup of tea as it would have been to have offered to pay the bania for his packet of cigarettes. So, as we leave this village, which is only one of the many thousands of similar villages scattered over the vast area viewed through your good field glasses from the top of Cheena, where I have spent the best part of my life, you can be assured that the welcome we received on arrival, and the invitation to return soon, are genuine expressions of the affection and goodwill of the people in my India for all who know and understand them.

2

Kunwar Singh

Kunwar Singh was by caste a Thakur, and the headman of Chandni Chauk village. Whether he was a good or a bad headman, I do not know. What endeared him to me was the fact that he was the best and the most successful poacher in Kaladhungi, and a devoted admirer of my eldest brother Tom, my boyhood's hero.

Kunwar Singh had many tales to tell of Tom, for he had accompanied him on many of his shikar expeditions, and the tale I like best, and that never lost anything in repetition, concerned an impromptu competition between brother Tom and a man by the name of Ellis, whom Tom had beaten by one point the previous year to win the B.P.R.A. gold medal for the best rifle-shot in India.

Tom and Ellis, unknown to each other, were shooting in the same jungle near Garuppu, and early one morning, when the mist was just rising above the tree tops, they met on the approach to some high ground overlooking a wide depression in which, at that hour of the morning, deer and pig were always to be found. Tom was accompanied by Kunwar Singh, while Ellis was accompanied by a shikari from Nainital named Budhoo, whom Kunwar Singh despised because of his low caste and his ignorance of all matters connected with the jungles.

After the usual greetings, Ellis said that, though Tom had beaten him by one miserable point on the rifle range, he would show Tom that he was a better game shot, and he suggested that they should each fire two shots to prove the point. Lots were drawn and Ellis, winning, decided to fire first. A careful approach was then made to the low ground, Ellis carrying the -450 Martini-Henry rifle with which he had competed at the B.P.R.A. meeting, while Tom carried a -400 D.B. express by Westley-Richards of which he was justly proud, for few of these weapons had, up to that date, arrived in India. The wind may have been wrong, or the approach careless. Anyway, when the competitors topped the high ground, no animals were in sight on the low ground.

On the near side of the low ground, there was a strip of dry grass beyond which the grass had been burnt, and it was on this burnt ground, now turning green with sprouting new shoots, that animals were to be seen both morning and evening. Kunwar Singh was of the opinion that some animals might be lurking in the strip of dry grass, and at his suggestion, he and Budhoo set fire to it.

When the grass was well alight and the drongos, rollers, and starlings were collecting from the four corners of the heavens to feed on the swarms of grasshoppers that were taking flight to escape from the flames, a movement was observed at the farther edge of the grass, and presently two big boars came out and went streaking across the burnt ground for the shelter of the tree jungle three hundred yards away. Very deliberately, Ellis, who weighed fourteen stone, knelt down, raised his rifle and sent a bullet after the hindmost pig, kicking up the dust between its hind legs. Lowering his rifle, Ellis adjusted the back sight to two hundred yards, ejected the spent cartridge, and rammed a fresh one into the breach. His second bullet sent up a cloud of dust immediately in front of the leading pig. This second bullet deflected the pigs to the right, bringing them broadside onto the guns, and making them increase their speed.

It was now Tom's turn to shoot, and to shoot in a hurry, for the pigs were fast approaching the tree jungle, and getting out of range. Standing four-square, Tom raised his rifle and, as the two shots rang out, the pigs, both shot through the head, went over like rabbits. Kunwar Singh's recital of this event invariably ended up with: 'And then I turned to Budhoo, that city-bred son of a low-caste man, the smell of whose oiled hair offended me, and said, "Did you see that, you, who boasted that your sahib would teach mine how to shoot? Had my sahib wanted to blacken the face of yours, he would not have used two bullets, but would have killed both pigs with one".'

Just how this feat could have been accomplished, Kunwar Singh never told me, and I never asked, for my faith in my hero was so great that I never, for one moment, doubted that, if he had wished, he could have killed both pigs with one bullet. Kunwar Singh was the first to visit me that day of days when I was given my first gun. He came early, and as with great pride I put the old double-barrelled muzzle-loader into his hands, he never, even by the flicker of an eyelid, showed that he had seen the gaping split in the right barrel, or the lappings of brass wire that held the stock and the barrels together. Only the good qualities of the left barrel were commented on, and extolled; its length, thickness, and the years of service it would give. And then, laying the gun aside, he turned to me and gladdened my eight-year-old heart and made me doubly proud of my possession by saying: 'You are now no longer a boy, but a man; and with this good gun you can go anywhere you like in our jungles and never be afraid, provided you learn how to climb trees.'

And I will now tell you a story to show how necessary it is for us men who shoot in the jungles to know how to do so. Har Singh and I went out to shoot one day last April, and all would have been well if a fox had not crossed our path as we were leaving the village. Har Singh, as you know, is a poor shikari with little knowledge of the jungle folk, and when, after seeing the fox, I suggested we should turn round and go home he laughed at me and said it was child's talk to say that a fox would bring us bad luck. So we continued on our way. We had started when the stars were paling, and near Garuppu I fired at a chital stag and unaccountably missed it. Later Har Singh broke the wing of a peafowl, but though we chased the wounded bird as hard as we could it got away in the long grass, where we lost it. Thereafter, though we combed the jungles we saw nothing to shoot, and towards the evening we turned our faces towards home.

Having fired two shots, and being afraid that the forest guards would be looking for us, we avoided the road and took a sandy nullah that ran through dense scrub and thorn-bamboo jungle. As we went along talking of our bad luck, suddenly a tiger came out into the nullah and stood looking at us. For a long minute the tiger stared and then it turned and went back the way it had come. After waiting a suitable time we continued on our way, when the tiger again came out into the nullah, and this time, as it stood and looked at us, it was growling and twitching its tail. We again stood quite still, and after a time the tiger quietened down and left the nullah. A little later a number of jungle fowl rose cackling out of the dense scrub, evidently disturbed by the tiger, and one of them came and sat on a haldu tree right in front of us. As the bird alighted on a branch in full view of us, Har Singh said he would shoot it and so avoid going home empty handed. He added that the shot would frighten away the tiger, and before I could stop him he fired.

Next second there was a terrifying roar as the tiger came crashing through the brushwood towards us. At this spot there were some runi trees growing on the edge of the nullah, and I dashed towards one while Har Singh dashed towards another. My tree was nearer to the tiger, but before it arrived I had climbed out of reach. Har Singh had not learnt to climb trees when a boy, as I had and he was still standing on the ground, reaching up and trying to grasp a branch, when the tiger, after leaving me, sprang at him.

The tiger did not bite or scratch Har Singh, but standing on its hind legs it clasped the tree, pinning Har Singh against it, and then started to claw big bits of bark and wood off the far side of the tree. While it was so engaged, Har Singh was screaming and the tiger was roaring. I had taken my gun up into the tree with me, so now, holding on with my bare feet, I cocked the hammer and fired the gun off into the air. On hearing the shot so close to it the tiger bounded away, and Har Singh collapsed at the foot of the tree.

When the tiger had been gone some time, I climbed down very silently, and went to Har Singh. I found that one of the tiger's claws had entered his stomach and torn the lining from near his navel to within a few fingers' breadth of the backbone, and that all his inside had fallen out. Here was great trouble for me. I could not run away and leave Har Singh, and not having any experience in these matters, I did not know whether it would be best to try and put all that mass of inside back into Har Singh's stomach, or cut it off. I talked in whispers on this matter with Har Singh, for we were afraid that if the tiger heard us it would return and kill us, and Har Singh was of the opinion that his inside should be put back into his stomach.

So, while he lay on his back on the ground, I stuffed it all back, including the dry leaves and grass and bits of sticks that were sticking to it. I then wound my pugree round him, knotting it tight to keep everything from falling out again, and we set out on the seven-mile walk to our village, myself in front, carrying the two guns, while Har Singh walked behind. We had to go slowly, for Har Singh was holding the pugree in position, and on the way, night came on and Har Singh said he thought it would be better to go to the hospital at Kaladhungi than to our village, so I hid the guns, and we went the extra three miles to the hospital.

The hospital was closed when we arrived, but the doctor babu who lives near by was awake, and when he heard our story he sent me to call Aladia the tobacco seller, who is also postmaster at Kaladhungi and who receives five rupees pay per month from Government, while he lit a lantern and went to the hospital hut with Har Singh. When I returned with Aladia, the doctor had laid Har Singh on a string bed and, while Aladia held the lantern and I held the two pieces of flesh together, the doctor sewed up the hole in Har Singh's stomach. Thereafter the doctor, who is a very kind man of raw years and who refused to take the two rupees I offered him, gave Har Singh a drink of very good medicine to make him forget the pain in his stomach and we went home and found our women folk crying, for they thought we had been killed in the jungle by dacoits, or by wild animals. So you see, Sahib, how necessary it is for us men who shoot in the jungles to know how to climb trees, for if Har Singh had had someone to advise him when he was a boy, he would not have brought all that trouble on us.

The runi tree against which the tigress—who evidently had just given birth to cubs in that area, and who resented the presence of human beings—pinned Har Singh, was about eighteen inches thick, and in her rage the tigress tore away a third of it. This tree became a landmark for all who shot or poached in the Garuppu jungles until, some twenty-five years later; it was destroyed by a forest fire. Har Singh, in spite of the rough and ready treatment he received at the hands of his three friends, and in spite of the vegetation that went inside him, suffered no ill effects from his wound, and lived to die of old age.

I learnt many things from Kunwar Singh during the first few years that I carried the old muzzle-loader, one of them being the making of mental maps. The jungles we hunted in, sometimes together, but more often alone—for Kunwar Singh had a horror of dacoits and there were times when for weeks on end he would not leave his village—were many hundreds of miles square with only one road running through them. Times without number, when returning from a shoot, I called in at Kunwar Singh's village, which was three miles nearer the forest than my house was, to tell him I had shot a chital or sambhar stag, or maybe a big pig, and to ask him to retrieve the bag.

He never once failed to do so, no matter in how great a wilderness of tree or scrub or grass jungle I had carefully hidden the animal I had shot, to protect it from vultures. We had a name for every outstanding tree, and for every water hole, game track and nullah. All our distances were measured by the imaginary flight of a bullet fired from a muzzle- loader, and all our directions fixed by the four points of the compass. When I had hidden an animal, or Kunwar Singh had seen vultures collected on a tree and suspected that a leopard or a tiger had made a kill, either he or I would set out with absolute, confidence that we would find the spot indicated, no matter what time of day or night it might be.

After I left school and started work in Bengal, I was only able to visit Kaladhungi for about three weeks each year, and I was greatly distressed to find on one of these annual visits that my old friend Kunwar Singh had fallen a victim to the curse of our foothills, opium. With a constitution weakened by malaria, the pernicious habit grew on him, and though he made me many promises, he had not the moral strength to keep them. I was therefore not surprised, on my visit to Kaladhungi one February, to be told by the men in our village that Kunwar Singh was very seriously ill. News of my arrival spread through Kaladhungi that night, and next day Kunwar Singh's youngest son, a lad of eighteen, came hot-foot to tell me that his father was at death's door, and that he wished to see me before he died.

As headman of Chandni Chauk, paying Government land revenue of four thousand rupees, Kunwar Singh was an important person, and lived in a big stone-built house with a slate roof in which I had often enjoyed his hospitality. Now as I approached the village in company with his son, I heard the wailing of women coming, not from the house, but from a small one-roomed hut Kunwar Singh had built for one of his servants. As the son led me towards the hut, he said his father had been moved to it because the grandchildren disturbed his sleep. Seeing us coming, Kunwar Singh's eldest son stepped out of the hut and informed me that his father was unconscious, and that he only had a few minutes to live. I stopped at the door of the hut, and when my eyes had got accustomed to the dim light, made dimmer by a thick pall of smoke which filled the room, I saw Kunwar Singh lying on the bare mud floor, naked, and partly covered with a sheet. His nerveless right arm was supported by an old man sitting on the floor near him, and his fingers were being held round the tail of a cow. This custom of a dying man being made to hold the tail of a cow—preferably that of a black heifer—has its origin in the Hindu belief that when the spirit leaves its earthly body it is confronted with a river of blood, on the far side of which sits the Judge before whom the spirit must appear to answer for its sins. The heifer's tail is the only way by which the departing spirit can cross the river, and if the spirit is not provided with means of transit it is condemned to remain on earth, to be a torment to those who failed to enable it to appear before the judgment seat.

Near Kunwar Singh's head was a brazier with cow-dung cakes burning on it, and by the brazier, a priest was sitting, intoning prayers and ringing a bell. Every available inch of floor space was packed with men, and with women who were wailing and repeating over and over again, 'He has gone! He has gone!' I knew men died like this in India every day, but I was not going to let my friend be one of them. In fact, if I could help it, he would not die at all, and anyway not at present. Striding into the room, I picked up the iron brazier, which was hotter than I expected it to be, and burnt my hands. This I carried to the door and flung outside. Returning, I cut the bark rope by which the cow was tethered to a peg driven into the mud floor, and led it outside.

As these acts, which I had performed in silence, became evident to the people assembled in the room, the hubbub began to die down, and it ceased altogether when I took the priest's arm and conducted him from the room. Then, standing at the door, I ordered everyone to go outside; the order was obeyed without a murmur or a single protest. The number of people, both old and young, who emerged from the hut, was incredible. When the last of them had crossed the doorstep, I told Kunwar Singh's eldest son to warm two seers of fresh milk and to bring it to me with as little delay as possible. The man looked at me in blank surprise, but when I repeated the order he hurried off to execute it. I now re- entered the hut, pulled forward a string bed which had been pushed against the wall, picked Kunwar Singh up and laid him on it.

Fresh air, and plenty of it, was urgently needed, and as I looked round I saw a small window which had been boarded up. It did not take long to tear down the boards and let a stream of clean sweet air blow directly from the jungles into the overheated room which reeked with the smell of human beings, cow dung, burnt ghee and acrid smoke. When I picked up Kunwar Singh's wasted frame, I knew there was a little life in it, but only a very little. His eyes, which were sunk deep into his head, were closed, his lips were blue, and his breath was coming in short gasps.

Soon, however, the fresh, clean air began to revive him and his breathing became less laboured and more regular, and presently, as I sat on his bed and watched through the door the commotion that was taking place among the mourners whom I had ejected from the death-chamber, I became aware that he had opened his eyes and was looking at me, and without turning my head, I began to speak. 'times have changed, uncle, and you, with them. There was a day when no man would have dared to remove you from your own house, and lay you on the ground in a servant's hut to die like an outcaste and a beggar. You would not listen to my words of warning and now the accursed drug has brought you to this. Had I delayed but a few minutes in answering your summons this day, you know you would by now have been on your way to the burning-ghat. As headman of Chandni Chauk and the best shikari in Kaladhungi, all men respected you. But now you have lost that respect, and you who were strong, and who ate of the best, are weak and empty of stomach, for as we came your son told me nothing has passed your lips for sixteen days. But you are not going to die, old friend, as they told you were. You will live for many more years, and though we may never shoot together again in the Garuppu jungles, you will not want for game, for I will share all I shoot with you, as I have always done. And now, here in this hut, with the sacred thread round your fingers and a pipal leaf in your hands, you must swear an oath on your eldest son's head that never again will you touch the foul drug. And this time you will and you shall keep your oath. And now, while we wait for the milk your son is bringing, we will smoke.'

Kunwar Singh had not taken his eyes off me while I was speaking and now for the first time he opened his lips and said, 'How can a man who is dying, smoke?' 'On the subject of dying,' I said, 'we will say no more, for as I have just told you, you are not going to die. And as to how we will smoke, I will show you.' Then, taking two cigarettes from my case, I lit one and placed it between his lips. Slowly he took a pull at it, coughed, and with a very feeble hand removed the cigarette. But when the fit of coughing was over, he replaced it between his lips and continued to draw on it. Before we had finished our smoke, Kunwar Singh's son returned carrying a big brass vessel, which he would have dropped at the door if I had not hurriedly relieved him of it. His surprise was understandable, for the father whom he had last seen lying on the ground dying, was now lying on the bed, his head resting on my hat, smoking. There was nothing in the hut to drink from, so I sent the son back to the house for a cup, and when he had brought it I gave Kunwar Singh a drink of warm milk.

I stayed in the hut till late into the night, and when I left Kunwar Singh had drunk a seer of milk and was sleeping peacefully on a warm and comfortable bed. Before I left, I warned the son that he was, on no account, to allow anyone to come near the hut, that he was to sit by his father and give him a drink of milk every time he awoke, and that if on my return in the morning I found Kunwar Singh dead, I would burn down the village. The sun was just rising next morning when I returned to Chandni Chauk to find both Kunwar Singh and his son fast asleep and the brass vessel empty. Kunwar Singh kept his oath, and though he never regained sufficient strength to accompany me on my shikar expeditions, he visited me often and died peacefully four years later in his own house and on his own bed.

3

Mothi

Mothi had the delicate, finely chiselled features that are the heritage of all high-caste people in India, but he was only a young stripling, all arms and legs, when his father and mother died and left him with the responsibilities of the family. Fortunately it was a small one, consisting only of his younger brother and sister. Mothi was at that time fourteen years of age, and had been married for six years. One of his first acts on finding himself unexpectedly the head of the family was to fetch his twelve-year-old wife—whom he had not seen since the day of their wedding—from her father's house in the Kota Dun, some dozen miles from Kaladhungi. As the cultivation of the six acres of land Mothi inherited, entailed more work than the four young people could tackle, Mothi took on a partner, locally known as Agee, who in return for his day-and-night services, received free board and lodging and half of the crops produced. The building of the communal hut with bamboos and grass procured from the jungles, under permit, and carried long distances on shoulder and on head, and the constant repairs to the hut necessitated by the violent storms that sweep the foothills, threw a heavy burden on Mothi and his helpers, and to relieve them of this burden I built them a masonry house with three rooms and a wide veranda, on a four-foot plinth. For, with the exception of Mothi's wife who had come from a higher altitude, all of them were steeped in malaria.

To protect their crops, the tenants used to erect a thorn fence round the entire village, but though it entailed weeks of hard labour, this flimsy fence afforded little protection against stray cattle and wild animals, and when the crops were on the ground, the tenants or members of their families, had to keep watch in the fields all night. Firearms were strictly rationed, and for our forty tenants, the Government allowed us one single-barrelled, muzzle-loading gun. This gun enables one tenant in turn to protect his crops with a lethal weapon, while the others had to rely on tin cans which they beat throughout the night. Though the gun accounted for a certain number of pigs and porcupines, which were the worst offenders, the nightly damage was considerable, for the village was isolated and surrounded by forests. So, when my handling contract at Mokameh Ghat began paying a dividend, I started building a masonry wall round the village. When completed, the wall was six-feet high and three miles long. It took ten years to build, for my share of the dividends was small. If today you motor from Haldwani to Ramnagar, through Kaladhungi, you will skirt the upper end of the wall before you cross the Boar Bridge and enter the forest.

I was walking through the village one cold December morning, with Robin, my dog, running ahead and putting up covey after covey of grey partridge which no one but Robin ever disturbed—for all who lived in the village loved to hear them calling at sunrise and at sunset—when in the soft ground at the edge of one of the irrigation channels I saw the tracks of a pig. This pig, with great, curved, wicked-looking tusks, was as big as a buffalo calf and was known to everyone in the village. As a squeaker he had wormed his way through the thorn fence and fattened on the crops. The wall had worried him at first, but it had a rough face and, being a determined pig, he had in time learnt to climb it. Time and time again the watchers in the fields had fired at him and on several occasions he had left a blood trail, but none of his wounds had proved fatal and the only effect they had had on him was to make him more wary.

On this December morning the pig's tracks led me towards Mothi's holding, and as I approached the house I saw Mothi's wife standing in front of it, her hands on her hips, surveying the ruin of their potato patch. The pig had done a very thorough job, for the tubers were not mature and he had been hungry, and while Robin cast round to see in which direction the marauder had gone, the woman gave vent to her feelings. 'It is all Punwa's father's fault', she said. 'It was his turn for the gun last night, and instead of staying at home and looking after his own property he must need go and sit up in Kalu's wheat field because he thought there was a chance of shooting a sambhar there. And while he was away, this is what the shaitan has done.' No woman in our part of India ever refers to her husband, or addresses him, by name. Before children are born he is referred to as the man of the house, and after children come is spoken of and addressed as the father of the firstborn. Mothi now had three children, of whom the eldest was Punwa, so to his wife he was 'Punwa's father', and his wife to everyone in the village was 'Punwa's mother'.

Punwa's mother was not only the hardest-working woman in our village but she also had the sharpest tongue, and after telling me in no uncertain terms what she thought of Punwa's father for having absented himself the previous night, she turned on me and said I had wasted my money in building a wall over which a pig could climb to eat her potatoes, and that if I could not shoot the pig myself, it was my duty to raise the wall a few feet so that no pig could climb over it. Mothi fortunately arrived while the storm was still breaking over my head, so whistling to Robin, I beat a hasty retreat and left him to weather it.

That evening I picked up the tracks of the pig on the far side of the wall and followed them for two miles, at times along game paths and at times along the bank of the Boar River, until they led me to a dense patch of thorn bushes interlaced with lantana. At the edge of this cover I took up position, as there was a fifty-fifty chance of the pig leaving the cover while there was still sufficient light for me to shoot by. Shortly after I had taken up position behind a rock on the bank of the river, a sambhar hind started belling at the upper end of the jungle in which a few years later, I was to shoot the Bachelor of Powalgarh. The hind was warning the jungle folk of the presence of a tiger. A fortnight previously, a party of three guns, with eight elephants, had arrived in Kaladhungi with the express purpose of shooting a tiger which, at that time, had his headquarters in the forest block for which I had a shooting pass.

The Boar River formed the boundary between my block and the block taken by the party of three guns, and they had enticed the tiger to kill in their block by tying up fourteen young buffaloes on their side of the river. Two of these buffaloes had been killed by the tiger, the other twelve had died of neglect, and at about nine o'clock the previous night I had heard the report of a heavy rifle. I sat behind the rock for two hours, listening to the belling sambhar but without seeing anything of the pig, and when there was no longer any light to shoot by, I crossed the river and, gaining the Kota road, loped down it, easing up and moving cautiously when passing the caves in which a big python lived, and where Bill Bailey of the Forest Department a month previously had shot a twelve-foot hamadryad. At the village gate I stopped and shouted to Mothi to be ready to accompany me at crack of dawn next morning.

Mothi had been my constant companion in the Kaladhungi jungles for many years. He was keen and intelligent, gifted with good eyesight and hearing, could move through the jungles silently, and was as brave as man could be. He was never late for an appointment, and as we walked through the dew-drenched jungle that morning, listening to the multitude of sounds of the awakening jungle folk, I told him of the belling of the sambhar hind and of my suspicion that she had witnessed the killing of her young one by the tiger, and that she had stayed to watch the tiger on his kill—a not uncommon occurrence—for in no other way could I account for her sustained belling.

Mothi was delighted at the prospect of our finding a fresh kill, for his means only permitted of his buying meat for his family once a month, and a sambhar, chital, or pig, freshly killed by a tiger or by a leopard, was a godsend to him. I had located the belling sambhar as being due north and some fifteen hundred yards from me the previous evening, and when we arrived at this spot and found no kill we started looking on the ground for blood, hair, or a drag mark that would lead us to the kill; for I was still convinced that there was a kill to be found and that the killer was a tiger.

At this spot two shallow depressions, coming down from the foot of the hill a few hundred yards away, met. The depressions ran more or less parallel to each other at a distance of about thirty yards and Mothi suggested that he should go up the right-hand depression while I went up the other. As there were only low bushes between, and we should be close to, and within sight of, each other, I agreed to the suggestion.

We had proceeded a hundred yards examining every foot of the ground, and going dead slow, when Mothi, just as I turned my head to look at him started backwards, screaming as he did so. Then he whipped round and ran for dear life, beating the air with his hands as if warding off a swarm of bees and continuing to scream as he ran. The sudden and piercing scream of a human being in a jungle where a moment before all has been silent is terrifying to hear, and quite impossible to describe. Instinctively I knew what had happened. With his eyes fixed on the ground, looking for blood or hair, Mothi had failed to see where he was going, and had walked on to the tiger. Whether he had been badly mauled or not I could not see, for only his head and shoulders were visible above the bushes. I kept the sights of my rifle a foot behind him as he ran, intending to press the trigger if I saw any movement, but to my intense relief there was no movement as I swung round, and after he had covered a hundred yards. I considered he was safe. I yelled to him to stop, adding that I was coming to him, then, backing away for a few yards, for I did not know whether the tiger had changed his position, I hurried down the depression towards Mothi. He was standing with his back against a tree and I was greatly relieved to see that there was no blood on him or on the ground on which he was standing. As I reached him he asked what had happened, and when I told him that nothing had happened, he expressed great surprise. He asked if the tiger had not sprung at him, or followed him, and when I replied that he had done everything possible to make the tiger do so, he said, 'I know, Sahib. I know I should not have screamed and run, but I—could—not—help—' as his voice tailed away and his head came forward, I caught him by the throat, but he slipped through my hands and slumped to the ground. Every drop of blood had drained from his face, and as he lay minute after long minute without any movement, I feared the shock had killed him.

There is little one can do in the jungles in an emergency of this kind, and that little I did. I stretched Mothi on his back, loosened his clothes, and massaged the region of his heart. Just as I was giving up hope and preparing to carry him home, he opened his eyes.

When Mothi was comfortably seated on the ground with his back to the tree and a half-smoked cigarette between his lips, I asked him to tell me exactly what had happened.

'I had gone a short distance up the depression after I left you', he said, 'closely examining the ground for traces of blood or hair, when I saw what looked like a spot of dry blood on a leaf. So I stooped down to have a closer look and, as I raised my head, I looked straight into the face of the tiger. The tiger was lying crouched down facing me at a distance of three or four paces. His head was a little raised off the ground, his mouth was wide open, and there was blood on his chin and on his chest. He looked as though he was on the point of springing at me, so I lost my head and screamed and ran away.

He had seen nothing of the sambhar kill. He said the ground was open and free of bushes and there was no kill where the tiger was lying.

Telling Mothi to stay where he was I stubbed out my cigarette and set off to investigate, for I could think of no reason why a tiger with its mouth open, and blood on its chin and on its chest, should allow Mothi to approach within a few feet, over open ground, and not kill him when he screamed in its face. Going with the utmost caution to the spot where Mothi was standing when he screamed, I saw in front of me a bare patch of ground from which the tiger had swept the carpet of dead leaves as he had rolled from side to side; at the nearer edge of this bare patch of ground there was a semicircle of clotted blood. Skirting round where the tiger had been lying, to avoid disturbing the ground, I picked up on the far side of it a light and fresh blood trail, which for no apparent reason zigzagged towards the hill, and then continued along the foot of the hill for a few hundred yards and entered a deep and narrow ravine in which there was a little stream. Up this ravine, which ran deep into the foothills, the tiger had gone. I made my way back to the bare patch of ground and examined the clotted blood. There were splinters of bone and teeth in it, and these splinters provided me with the explanation I was looking for. The rifle-shot I had heard two nights previously had shattered the tiger's lower jaw, and he had made for the jungle in which he had his home. He had gone as far as his sufferings and loss of blood permitted and had then lain down on the spot where first the sambhar had seen him tossing about, and where thirty hours later Mothi walked on to him.

The most painful wound that can be inflicted on an animal, the shattering of the lower jaw, had quite evidently induced high fever and the poor beast had perhaps only been semi-conscious when he heard Mothi screaming in his face. He had got up quietly and staggered away, in a last effort to reach the ravine in which he knew there was water.

To make quite sure that my deductions were correct, Mothi

and I crossed the river into the adjoining shooting block to have a look at the ground where the fourteen buffaloes had been tied up. Here, high up in a tree, we found the machan the three guns had sat on, and the kill the tiger had been eating when fired at. From the kill, a heavy blood trail led down to the river, with elephant tracks on each side of it. Leaving Mothi on the right bani I recrossed the river into my block, picked up the blood trail and the elephant tracks, and followed them for five or six hundred yards to where the trail led into heavy cover. At the edge of the cover where the elephants had halted and, after standing about for some time, had turned to the right and gone away in the direction of Kaladhungi. I had met the returning elephants as I was starting out the previous evening to try and get a shot at the old pig, and one of the guns had asked me where I was going, and when I told him, had appeared to want to tell me something but was restrained from doing so by his companions. So, while the party of three guns went off on their elephants to the Forest Bungalow where they were staying, I had gone off on foot, without any warning, into the jungle in which they had left a wounded tiger.

The walk back to the village from where I had left Mothi was only about three miles, but it took us about as many hours to cover the distance, for Mothi was unaccountably weak and had to rest frequently. After leaving him at his house I went straight to the Forest Bungalow, where I found the party of three packed up and on the point of leaving to catch the evening train at Haldwani. We talked on the steps of the veranda for some little time, I doing most of the talking, and when I learnt that the only reason they could not spare the time to recover the tiger they had wounded was the keeping of a social engagement. I told them that if Mothi died as a result of shock or if the tiger killed any of my tenants, they would have to face a charge of manslaughter.

The party left after my talk with them, and next morning, armed with a heavy rifle, I entered the ravine up which the tiger had gone, not with the object of recovering a trophy for others, but with the object of putting the tiger out of his misery and burning his skin. The ravine, every foot of which I knew, was the last place I would have selected in which to look for a wounded tiger. However, I searched it from top to bottom, and also the hills on either side, for the whole of that day without finding any trace of the tiger, for the blood trail had stopped shortly after he entered the ravine.

Ten days later, a forest guard on his rounds came on the remains of a tiger that had been eaten by vultures. In the summer of that year, the Government made a rule prohibiting sitting up for tigers between the hours of sunset and sunrise, and making it incumbent on sportsmen wounding tigers to make every effort to bring the wounded animal to bag, and to make an immediate report of the occurrence to the nearest Forest Officer and police outpost. Mothi met with his experience in December, and when we left Kaladhungi in April he appeared to be little the worse for the shock. But his luck was out, for a month later be was badly mauled by a leopard he wounded one night in his field and followed next morning into heavy covers, and he had hardly recovered from his wounds when he had the misfortune of being responsible for the death of a cow—the greatest crime a Hindu can commit.

The cow, an old and decrepit animal that had strayed in from an adjoining village, was grazing in Mothi's field, and as he attempted to drive it out it, put its hoof in a deep rat-hole and broke its leg. For weeks Mothi attended assiduously to the cow as it lay in his field, but it died eventually, and the matter being too serious for the village priest to deal with, he ordered Mothi to make a pilgrimage to Haridwar. So, having borrowed money for the journey, to Haridwar Mothi went. Here to the head priest at the main temple Mothi, confessed his crime, and after that dignitary had given the offence due consideration he ordered Mothi to make a donation to the temple: this would absolve him of his crime, but in order to show repentance he would have also to do penance. The priest then asked him from what acts he derived most pleasure and Mothi, being without guile, made answer that he derived most pleasure from shooting, and from eating meat. Mothi was then told by the priest that in future he must refrain from these two pleasures.

Mothi returned from his pilgrimage cleared of his crime, but burdened with a lifelong penance. His opportunities for shooting had been few, for besides having to share the muzzle-loading gun with others he had had to confine his shooting to the village boundaries, as no man in his position was permitted to shoot in Government forests. Even so, Mothi had derived great pleasure from the old gun, and from the occasional shots I had permitted him—against all rules— to fire from my rifle. Hard as this half of his penance was, the second half was even harder, and, moreover, it adversely affected his health. Though his means had only allowed him to buy a small meat ration once a month, pigs and porcupines were plentiful, and deer occasionally strayed into the fields at night. It was the custom in our village, a custom to which I also adhered, for an animal shot by one to be shared by all, so Mothi had not had to depend entirely on the meat he could buy.

It was during the winter following his pilgrimage to Haridwar that Mothi developed a hacking cough. As the remedies we tried failed to give relief, I got a doctor friend who was passing through Kaladhungi to examine him, and was horrified to learn that he was suffering from tuberculosis.

On the doctor's recommendation I sent Mothi to the Bhowali Sanatorium, thirty miles away. Five days later he returned with a letter from the Superintendent of the Sanatorium saying that the case was hopeless, and that for this reason, the Superintendent regretted he could not admit Mothi. A medical missionary who was staying with us at the time, and who had worked for years in a sanatorium, advised us to make Mothi sleep in the open and drink a quart of milk with a few drops of paraffin in it each morning.

So for the rest of that winter Mothi slept in the open, and while sitting on our veranda, smoking a cigarette and talking to me, each morning drank a quart of milk, fresh from our cows.

The poor of India are fatalists, and in addition have little stamina to fight disease. Deprived of our company, though not of our help, Mothi lost hope when we left for our summer home, and died a month later.

The women of our foothills are the hardest workers in India, and the hardest working of them all was Mothi's widow, Punwa's mother. A small, compact woman, as hard as flint and a beaver for work—young enough to remarry but precluded from doing so by reasons of her caste—she bravely and resolutely faced the future, and right gallantly she fulfilled her task, ably assisted by her young children. Of her three children, Punwa, the eldest, was now twelve, and with the assistance of neighbours, was able to do the ploughing and other field jobs.

Kunthi, a girl, was ten and married, and until she left the village five years later to join her husband she assisted her mother in all her thousand and one tasks, which included cooking the food and washing up the dishes; washing and mending the clothes—for Punwa's mother was very particular about her own and her children's dress, and no matter how old and patched the garments were, they always had to be clean; fetching water from the irrigation furrow or from the Boar river for domestic purposes; bringing firewood from the jungles, and grass and tender young leaves for the milch, cows and their calves; weeding and cutting the crops; husking the paddy, in a hole cut in a slab of rock, with an iron shod staff that was heavy enough to tire the muscles of any man; winnowing the wheat for Punwa to take to the watermill to be ground into atta; and making frequent visits to the bazaar two miles away to drive hard bargains for the few articles of food and clothing the family could afford to buy. Sher Singh, the youngest child, was eight, and from the moment he opened his eyes at crack of dawn each morning until he closed them when the evening meal had been eaten, he did everything that a boy could do. He even gave Punwa a hand with the ploughing, though he had to be helped at the end of each furrow as he was not strong enough to turn the plough.

Sher Singh, without a care in the world, was the happiest child in the village. When he could not be seen, he could always be heard, for he loved to sing. The cattle—four bullocks, twelve cows, eight calves, and Lalu the bull—were his special charge, and each morning after milking the cows, he released the herd from the stakes to which he had tethered them the evening before, drove them out of the shed and through a wicket in the boundary wall, and then set to clean up the shed. It would now be time for the morning meal, and when he heard the call from his brother, or Kunthi, he would hurry home across the fields taking the milk can with him. The frugal morning meal consisted of fresh hot chapatis and dal, liberally seasoned with green chillies and salt and cooked in mustard oil. Having breakfasted, and finished any chores about the house that he was called upon to do, Sher Singh would begin his day's real work. This was to graze the cattle in the jungle, prevent them from straying, and guard them against leopards and tigers. Having collected the four bullocks and twelve cows from the open ground beyond the boundary wall, where they would be lying basking in the sun, and left Kunthi to keep an eye on the calves, this small tousle-headed boy, his axe over his shoulder and Lalu the bull following him, would drive his charges over the Boar Bridge and into the dense jungle beyond, calling to each by name.

Lalu was a young scrub bull destined to be a plough-bullock when he had run his course but who, at the time I am writing about, was free of foot and the pride of Sher Singh his foster- brother, for Lalu had shared his mother's milk with Sher Singh. Sher Singh had christened his foster-brother *Lalu,* which means red. But Lalu was not red. He was of a light dun colour, with stronger markings on the shoulders and a dark, almost black line running down the length of his back. His horns were short, sharp, and strong, with the light and dark colourings associated with the shoehorns that adorned dressing tables of that period.

When human beings and animals live in close association with each other under conditions in which they are daily subjected to common dangers, each infuses the other with a measure of courage and confidence which the one possesses and the other lacks. Sher Singh, whose father and grandfather had been more at home in the jungles than in the walks of men, had no fear of anything that walked, and Lalu, young and vigorous, had unbounded confidence in himself. So while Sher Singh infused Lalu with courage, Lalu in turn infused Sher Singh with confidence. In consequence Sher Singh's cattle grazed where others feared to go, and he was justly proud of the fact that they were in better condition than any others in the village, and that no-leopard or tiger had ever taken toll of them.

Four miles from our village there is a valley about five miles in length, running north and south, which has no equal in beauty or richness of wild life in the five thousand square miles of forest land in the United Provinces. At the upper end of the valley a clear stream, which grows in volume as it progresses, gushes from a cave in which a python lives, from under the roots of an old jamun tree. This crystal-clear stream with its pools and runs is alive with many kinds of small fish on which live no fewer than five varieties of kingfishers.

In the valley grow flowering and fruit-bearing trees and bushes that attract a multitude of nectar-drinking and fruit-eating birds and animals, which in turn attract predatory birds and carnivorous animals which find ample cover in the dense undergrowth and matted cane-brakes. In places the set of the streamhas caused miniature landslides, and on these grows a reedy kind of grass, with broad lush leaves, much fancied by sambhar and kakar.

The valley was a favourite haunt of mine. One winter–evening, shortly after our descent to Kaladhungi from our summer home, I was standing at a point where there is a clear view into the valley when, in a clump of grass to the left, I saw a movement. After a long scrutiny the movement revealed itself as an animal feeding on the lush grass on a steep slope. The animal was too light for a sambhar and too big for a kakar, so I set out to stalk it, and as I did so a tiger started calling in the valley a few hundred yards lower down. My quarry also heard the tiger, and as it raised its head I saw to my surprise that it was Lalu. With head poised he stood perfectly still listening to the tiger, and when it stopped calling, he unconcernedly resumed cropping the grass. This was forbidden ground for Lalu, for cattle are not permitted to graze in Government Reserved Forests, and moreover Lalu was in danger from the tiger; so I called to him by name and, after a little hesitation, he came up the steep bank and we returned to the village together. Sher Singh was tying up his cattle in the shed when we arrived, and when I told him where I had found Lalu he laughed and said, 'Don't fear for this one, Sahib. The forest guard is a friend of mine and would not impound my Lalu, and as for the tiger, Lalu is well able to take care of himself.'

Not long after this incident, the Chief Conservator of Forests, Smythies, and his wife arrived on tour in Kaladhungi, and as the camels carrying their camp equipment were coming down the forest road towards the Boar Bridge, a tiger killed a cow on the road in front of them. On the approach of the camels, and the shouting of the men with them, the tiger left the cow on the road and bounded into the jungle. The Smythies were sitting on our veranda having morning coffee when the camel men brought word of the killing of the cow. Mrs Smythies was keen to shoot the tiger, so I went off with two of her men to put up a machan for her, and found that in the meantime the tiger had returned and dragged the cow twenty yards into the jungle. When the machan was ready I sent back for Mrs Smythies and, after putting her into the machan with a forest guard to keep her company, I climbed a tree on the edge of the road hoping to get a photograph of the tiger.

It was 4 p.m. We had been in position half an hour and a kakar had just started barking in the direction in which we knew the tiger was lying up, when down the road came Lalu. On reaching the spot where the cow had been killed he very carefully smelt the ground and a big pool of blood, then turned to the edge of the road and with head held high and nose stretched out started to follow the drag. When he saw the cow he circled round her, tearing up the ground with his hoofs and snorting with rage. After tying my camera to a branch I slipped off the tree and conducted a very angry and protesting Lalu to the edge of the village. Hardly had I returned to my perch on the tree, however, when up the road came Lalu to make a second demonstration round the dead cow. Mrs Smythies now sent the forest guard to drive Lalu away, and as the man passed me I told him to take the bull across the Boar Bridge and to remain there with the elephant that was coming later for Mrs Smythies.

The kakar had stopped barking some time previously and a covey of jungle fowl now started cackling a few yards behind the machan. Getting my camera ready I looked towards Mrs Smythies, and saw she had her rifle poised, and at that moment Lalu appeared for the third time. (We learnt later that, after being taken across the bridge, he had circled round, crossed the river bed lower down and disappeared into the jungle.) This time Lalu trotted up to the cow and, either seeing or smelling the tiger, lowered his head and charged into the bushes, bellowing loudly. Three times he did this, and after each charge he retreated backwards to his starting-point, slashing upwards with his horns as he did so.

I have seen buffaloes driving tigers away from their kills, and I have seen cattle doing the same with leopards but, with the exception of a Himalayan bear, I had never before seen a solitary animal—and a scrub bull at that— drive a tiger away from his kill.

Courageous as Lalu was, he was no match for the tiger, who was now losing his temper and answering Lalu's bellows with angry growls. Remembering a small boy back in the village whose heart would break if anything happened to his beloved companion, I was on the point of going to Lalu's help when Mrs Smythies very sportingly gave up her chance of shooting the tiger, so I shouted to the mahout to bring up the elephant. Lalu was very subdued as he followed me to the shed where Sher Singh was waiting to tie him up, and I think he was as relieved as I was that the tiger had not accepted his challenge while he was defending the dead cow.

The tiger fed on the cow that night and next evening, and while Mrs Smythies was having another unsuccessful try to get a shot at him, I took a nice picture which some who read this story, may remember having seen.

In the picture, the tiger is seen coming down a steep bank, and drinking at a little pool.

The jungle was Sher Singh's playground, the only playground he ever knew, just as it had been my playground as a boy, and of all whom I have known, he alone enjoyed the jungles as much as I have done. Intelligent and observant, his knowledge of jungle lore was incredible. Nothing escaped his attention, and he was as fearless as the animal whose name he bore.

Our favourite evening walk was along one of the three roads which met on the far side of the Boar Bridge—the abandoned trunk road to Moradabad, the road to Kota, and the forest road to Ramnagar. Most evenings at sundown we would hear Sher Singh before we saw him, for he sang with abandon in a clear treble voice that carried far as he drove his cattle home. Always he would greet us with a smile and a salaam, and always he would have something interesting to tell us.

'the big tiger's tracks were on the road this morning coming from the direction of Kota and going towards Naya Gaon, and at midday I heard him calling at the lower end of the Dhunigad cane-brake.' 'Near Saryapani I heard the clattering of horns, so I climbed a tree and saw two chital stags righting. One of them has very big horns, Sahib, and is very fat, and I have eaten no meat for many days.'

'What am I carrying?'—He had something wrapped in big green leaves and tied round with bark balanced on his tousled head. 'I am carrying a pig's leg. I saw some vultures on a tree, so I went to have a look and under a bush I found a pig killed by a leopard last night and partly eaten. If you want to shoot the leopard, Sahib, I will take you to the kill.' 'today I found a beehive in a hollow haldu tree', he said one day, proudly exhibiting a large platter of leaves held together with long thorns on which the snow-white comb was resting. 'I have brought the honey for you.' Then, glancing at the rifle in my hands, he added, 'I will bring the honey to the house when I have finished my work for perchance you may meet a pig or a kakar and with the honey in your hands you would not be able to shoot.' The cutting of the hive out of the haldu tree with his small axe had probably taken him two hours or more, and he had got badly stung in the process, for his hands were swollen and one eye was nearly closed, but he said nothing about this and to have commented on it would have embarrassed him.

Later that night, while we were having dinner, he slipped silently into the room and as he laid the brass tray, polished till it looked like gold, on our table, he touched the elbow of his right arm with the fingers of his left hand, an old hill custom denoting respect, which is fast dying out.

After depositing such a gift on the table, leaving the tray for Kunthi to call for in the morning, Sher Singh would pause at the door and, looking down and scratching the carpet with his toes, would say, 'If you are going bird shooting tomorrow I will send Kunthi out with the cattle and come with you, for I know where there are a lot of birds'. He was always shy in a house, and on these occasions, spoke with a catch in his voice as though he had too many words in his mouth and was trying, with difficulty, to swallow the ones that were getting in his way.

Sher Singh was in his element on these bird shoots, which the boys of the village enjoyed as much as he and I did, for in addition to the excitement and the prospect of having a bird to take home at the end of the day, there was always a halt at midday at a prearranged spot to which the man sent out earlier would bring the fresh sweets and parched gram that would provide a meal for all.

When I had taken my position, Sher Singh would line up his companions and beat the selected cover towards me, shouting the loudest of them all and worming his way through the thickest cover. When a bird was put up he would yell, 'It's coming, Sahib! It's coming!' Or when a heavy animal went crashing through the undergrowth, as very frequently happened, he would call to his companions not to run away, assuring them that it was only a sambhar, or a chital, or maybe a sounder of pig. Ten to twelve patches of cover would be beaten in the course of the day, yielding as many peafowl and jungle fowl, and two or three hares, and possibly a small pig or a porcupine. At the end of the last beat, the bag would be shared out among the beaters and the gun, or if the bag was small, only among the beaters, and Sher Singh was never more happy than when, at the end of the day, he made for home with a peacock in full plumage proudly draped over his shoulders.

Punwa was now married, and the day was fast approaching when Sher Singh would have to leave the home, for there was not sufficient room on the small holding of six acres for the two brothers. Knowing that it would break Sher Singh's heart to leave the village and his beloved jungles, I decided to apprentice him to a friend who had a garage at Kathgodam, and who ran a fleet of cars on the Nainital motor road.

After his training, it was my intention to employ Sher Singh to drive our car and accompany me on my shooting trips during the winter, and to look after our cottage and garden at Kaladhungi while we were in Nainital during the summer. Sher Singh was speechless with delight when I told him of the plans I had made for him, plans which ensured his continued residence in the village, and within sight and calling distance of the home he had never left from the day of his birth.

Plans a-many we make in life, and I am not sure there is cause for regret when some go wrong. Sher Singh was to have started his apprenticeship when we returned to Kaladhungi in

November. In October he contracted malignant malaria which led to pneumonia, and a few days before we arrived he died. During his boyhood's years he had sung through life, happy as the day was long and, had he lived, who can say that his life in a changing world would have been as happy, and as carefree, as those first few years?

Before leaving our home for a spell, to regain in new climes the health we lost in Hitler's war, I called together our tenants and their families as I had done on two previous occasions, to tell them the time had come for them to take over their holdings and run the village for themselves. Punwa's mother was the spokesman for the tenants on this occasion, and after I had had my say she got to her feet and, in her practical way, spoke as follows: 'You have called us away from our work to no purpose. We have told you before and we tell you again that we will not take your land from you, for to do so would imply that we were no longer your people. And now, Sahib, what about the pig, the son of the shaitan who climbed your wall and ate my potatoes? Punwa and these others cannot shoot it and I am tired of sitting up all night and beating a tin can.'

Maggie and I were walking along the fire-track that skirts the foothills with David at our heels when the pig—worthy son of the old shaitan who, full of years and pellets of buckshot, had been killed in an all-night fight with a tiger—trotted across the track.

The sun had set and the range was long—all of three hundred yards—but a shot was justifiable for the pig was quite evidently on his way to the village. I adjusted the sights and, resting the rifle against a tree, waited until the pig paused at the edge of a deep depression. When I pressed the trigger, the pig jumped into the depression, scrambled out on the far side, and made off at top speed. 'Have you missed him?' asked Maggie, and with his eyes, David put the same question. There was no reason, except miscalculation of the range, why I should not have hit the pig, for my silver foresight had shown up clearly on his black skin, and the tree had assisted me to take steady aim. Anyway, it was time to make for home, and as the cattle track down which the pig had been going would lead us to the Boar Bridge, we set off to see the result of my shot. The pig's feet had bitten deeply into the ground where he had taken off, and on the far side of the depression, where he had scrambled out, there was blood. Two hundred yards in the direction in which the pig had gone, there was a narrow strip of dense cover. I should probably find him dead in the morning in this cover, for the blood trail was heavy; but if he was not dead and there was trouble, Maggie would not be with me, and there would be more light to shoot by in the morning than there was now.

Punwa had heard my shot and was waiting on the bridge for us. 'Yes', I said, in reply to his eager inquiry, 'it was the old pig I fired at, and judging by the blood trail, he is hit hard.' I added that if he met me on the bridge next morning I would show him where the pig was, so that later he could take out a party of men to bring it in. 'May I bring the old havildar too?' said Punwa, and I agreed.

The havildar, a kindly old man who had won the respect and affection of all, was a Gurkha who, on leaving the army, had joined the police, and having retired a year previously, had settled down with his wife and two sons on a plot of land we had given him in our village. Like all Gurkhas, the havildar had an insatiable appetite for pig's flesh, and when a pig was shot by any of us, it was an understood thing that no matter who went short, the ex-soldier-policeman must have his share. Punwa and the havildar were waiting for me at the bridge next morning. Following the cattle track, we soon reached the spot where, the previous evening, I had seen the blood. From here we followed the well-defined blood trail which led us, as I had expected, to the dense cover. I left my companions at the edge of the cover, for a wounded pig is a dangerous animal, and with one exception—a bear—is the only animal in our jungles that has the unpleasant habit of savaging any human being who has the misfortune to be attacked and knocked down by him. For this reason, wounded pigs, especially if they have big tusks, have to be treated with great respect. The pig had stopped where I had expected him to, but he had not died, and at daybreak he had got up from where he had been lying all night and left the cover. I whistled to Punwa and the havildar and when they rejoined me, we set off to trail the animal.

The trail led us across the fire-track, and from the direction in which the wounded animal was going it was evident he was making for the heavy jungle on the far side of the hill, from which I suspected he had come the previous evening. The morning blood trail was light and continued to get lighter the farther we went, until we lost it altogether in a belt of trees, the fallen leaves of which a gust of wind had disturbed. In front of us at this spot was a tinder-dry stretch of waist-high grass. Still under the conviction that the pig was heading for the heavy jungle on the far side of the hill, I entered the grass, hoping to pick up the tracks again on the far side.

The havildar had lagged some distance behind, but Punwa was immediately behind me when, after we had gone a few yards into the grass, my woollen stockings caught on the thorns of a low bush. While I was stooping to free myself, Punwa, to avoid the thorns, moved a few paces to the right and I just got free and was straightening up, when out of the grass shot the pig and with an angry grunt went straight for Punwa, who was wearing a white shirt. I then did what I have always asked companions who have accompanied me into the jungles after dangerous game to do if they saw me attacked by a wounded animal. I threw the muzzle of my rifle into the air, and shouted at the top of my voice as I pressed the trigger.

If the thorns had not caught in my stockings and lost me a fraction of a second, all would have been well, for I should have killed the pig before it got to Punwa; but once the pig had reached him the only thing I could do to help him was to try to cause a diversion, for to have fired in his direction would further have endangered his life. As the bullet was leaving my rifle to land in the jungle a mile away, Punwa, with a despairing scream of 'sahib', was falling backwards into the grass with the pig right on top of him, but at my shout and the crack of the rifle the pig turned like a whiplash straight for me, and before I was able to eject the spent cartridge and ram a fresh one into the chamber of the ·275 rifle, he was at me. Taking my right hand from the rifle I stretched the arm out, palm downwards, and as my hand came in contact with his forehead he stopped dead, for no other reason than that my time had not come, for he was big and angry enough to have knocked over and savaged a cart horse. The pig's body had stopped but his head was very active, and as he cut upwards with his great tusks, first on one side and then on the other, fortunately cutting only the air, he wore the skin off the palm of my hand with his rough forehead. Then, for no apparent reason, he turned away, and as he made off, I put two bullets into him in quick succession and he pitched forward on his head.

After that one despairing scream Punwa had made no sound or movement, and with the awful thought of what I would say to his mother, and the still more awful thought of what she would say to me, I went with fear and trembling to where he was lying out of sight in the grass, expecting to find him ripped open from end to end. He was laying full stretch on his back, and his eyes were closed, but to my intense relief I saw no blood on his white clothes. I shook him by the shoulder and asked him how he was, and where he had been hurt. In a very weak voice he said he was dead, and that his back was broken.

I straddled his body and gently raised him to a sitting position, and was overjoyed to find that he was able to retain this position when I released my hold. Passing my hand down his back I assured him that it was not broken, and after he had verified this fact with his own hand, he turned his head and looked behind him to wherc a dry stump was projecting two or three inches above the ground. Evidently he had fainted when the pig knocked him over and, on coming to, feeling the stump boring into his back, had jumped to the conclusion that it was broken.

And so the old pig, son of the shaitan, died, and in dying, nearly frightened the lives out of two of us. But beyond rubbing a little skin off my hand he did us no harm, for Punwa escaped without a scratch and with a grand story to tell. The havildar, like the wise old soldier he was, had remained in the background. None the less, he claimed a lion's share of the pig, for had he not stood foursquare in reserve to render assistance if assistance had been called for? And further, was it not the custom for those present at a killing to receive a double share, and what difference was there between seeing and hearing the shots that had killed the pig? So a double share was not denied him, and he too, in the course of time, had a grand story to tell of the part he took in that morning's exploit.

Punwa now reigns, and is raising a family, in the house I built for his father. Kunthi has left the village to join her husband, and Sher Singh waits in the Happy Hunting Grounds. Punwa's mother is still alive, and if you stop at the village gate and walk through the fields to Punwa's house you will find her keeping house for Punwa and his family and working as hard and as cheerfully at her thousand and one tasks as she worked when she first came to our village as Mothi's bride. During the war years, Maggie spent the winters alone in our cottage at Kaladhungi, without transport, and fourteen miles from the nearest settlement. Her safety gave me no anxiety, for I knew she was safe among my friends, the poor of India.

4

Pre-Red-Tape Days

I was camping with Anderson one winter in the Terai, the low-lying stretch of country at the foot of the Himalayas, and having left Bindukhera after breakfast one morning in early January, we made a wide detour to Boksar, our next camping-place, to give our servants time to pack up and pitch our tents before our arrival.

There were two small unbridged rivers to cross between Bindukhera and Boksar, and at the second of these rivers one of the camels carrying our tents slipped on the clay bottom and deposited its load in the river. This accident resulted in a long delay, with the result that we arrived at Boksar, after a very successful day's black partridge shooting, while our kit was still being unloaded from the camels.

The camp site was only a few hundred yards from Boksar village, and as Anderson's arrival was a great event, the entire population had turned out to pay their respects to him and to render what assistance they could in setting up our camp.

Sir Frederick Anderson was at that time, Superintendent of the Terai and Bhabar Government Estates, and by reason of the large amount of the milk of human kindness that he was endowed with, he had endeared himself to the large population, embracing all castes and creeds, living in the many thousands of square miles of country he ruled over. In addition to his kindly nature, Anderson was a great administrator and was gifted with a memory which I have only seen equalled in one other man, General Sir Henry Ramsay, who for twenty-eight years, administered the same tract of country, and who throughout his service was known as the Uncrowned King of Kumaon. Both Ramsay and Anderson were Scotsmen, and it was said of them that once having heard a name or seen a face, they never forgot it. It is only those who have had dealings with simple uneducated people who can realize the value of a good memory, for nothing appeals so much to a humble man as the remembering of his name, or the circumstances in which he has previously been met.

When the history of the rise and fall of British Imperialism is written, due consideration will have to be given to the important part red tape played in the fall of the British raj. Both Ramsay and Anderson served India at a time when red tape was unknown, and their popularity and the success of their administration was in great measure due to their hands not being tied with it.

Ramsay, in addition to being Judge of Kumaon, was also magistrate, policeman, forest officer and engineer, and as his duties were manifold and onerous, he performed many of them while walking from one camp to another. It was his custom while on these long walks, and while accompanied by a crowd of people, to try all his civil and criminal cases. The complainant and his witnesses were first heard, and then the defendant and his witnesses, and after due deliberation, Ramsay would pronounce judgment, which might be either a fine or a sentence to imprisonment. In no case was his judgment known to be questioned, nor did any man whom he had sentenced to a fine or imprisonment, fail to pay the fine into the Government Treasury or fail to report himself at the nearest jail to carry out the term of simple or rigorous imprisonment to which Ramsay had sentenced him.

As Superintendent of the Terai and Bhabar, Anderson had only to perform a part of the duties that had been performed by his predecessor Ramsay, but he had wide administrative powers, and that afternoon, while our tents were being pitched on the camping ground at Boksar, Anderson told the assembled people to sit down, adding that he would listen to any complaints they had to make and receive any petitions they wished to present.

The first petition came from the headman of a village adjoining Boksar. It appeared that this village and Boksar had a joint irrigation channel that served both villages, and that ran through Boksar. Owing to the partial failure of the monsoon rains, the water in the channel had not been sufficient for both villages and Boksar village had used it all, with the result that the paddy crop of the lower village had been ruined. The headman of Boksar admitted that no water had been allowed to go down the channel to the lower village and justified his action by pointing out that, if the water had been shared, the paddy crops of both villages would have been ruined. The crop had been harvested and threshed a few days before our arrival, and after Anderson had heard what the two headmen had to say, he ordered that the paddy should be divided up according to the acreage of the two villages. The people of Boksar acknowledged the justice of this decision, but claimed they were entitled to payment of the labour that had been employed in harvesting and threshing the crop. To this claim, the lower village objected on the ground that no request had been made to them for help while the Boksar crop was being harvested and threshed. Anderson upheld the objection, and while the two headmen went off to divide the paddy, the next petition was presented to him.

This was from Chadi, accusing Kalu of having abducted his wife Tilni. Chadi's complaint was that three weeks previously, Kalu had made advances to Tilni; that in spite of his protests, Kalu had persisted in his advances; and that ultimately Tilni had left his hut and taken up residence with Kalu. When Anderson asked if Kalu was present, a man sitting at the edge of the semicircle in front of us, stood up and said he was Kalu.

While the case of the paddy had been under discussion, the assembled women and girls had shown little interest, for that was a matter to be decided by their menfolk. But this abduction case, judging from the expression on their faces and the sharp intakes of breath, was one in which they were all intensely interested.

When Anderson asked Kalu if he admitted the charge that Chadi had brought against him, he admitted that Tilni was living in the hut he had provided for her but he stoutly denied that he had abducted her. When asked if he was prepared to return Tilni to her lawful husband, Kalu replied that Tilni had come to him of her own free will and that he was not prepared to force her to return to Chadi. 'Is Tilni present?' asked Anderson. A girl from among the group of women came forward and said, 'I am Tilni. What does Your Honour want with me?'

Tilni was a clean-limbed, attractive young girl, some eighteen years of age. Her hair, done in a foot-high cone in the traditional manner of the women of the Terai, was draped with a white-bordered black sari, her upper person was encased in a tight-fitting red bodice, and a voluminous gaily coloured skirt completed her costume. When asked by Anderson why she had left her husband, she pointed to Chadi and said, 'Look at him. Not only is he dirty, as you can see, but he is also a miser, and during the two years I have been married to him he has not given me any clothes, nor has he given me any jewellery. These clothes that you are looking at and this jewellery', she said, touching some silver bangles on her wrists, and several strings of glass beads round her neck, 'were given to me by Kalu.' Asked if she was willing to go back to Chadi, Tilni tossed her head and said nothing would induce her to do so.

This aboriginal tribe, living in the unhealthy Terai, is renowned for two sterling qualities—cleanliness, and the independence of the women. In no other part of India are villages and the individual dwellings as spotlessly clean as they are in the Terai, and in no other part of India would a young girl have dared or in fact been permitted, to stand before a mixed gathering including two white men to plead her own cause. Chadi was now asked by Anderson if he had any suggestions to make, to which he replied: 'You are my mother and my father. I came to you for justice, and if Your Honour is not prepared to compel my wife to return to me, I claim compensation for her.' 'to what extent do you claim compensation for her?' asked Anderson, to which Chadi replied, 'I claim one hundred and fifty rupees'. From all sides of the semicircle there were now exclamations of 'He claims too much', 'far too much', and 'she is not worth it'. On being asked by Anderson if he was willing to pay one hundred and fifty rupees for Tilni, Kalu said the price demanded was excessive and added that he knew, as everyone in Boksar knew, that Chadi had only paid a hundred rupees for Tilni. This price, he argued, had been paid for Tilni when she was 'new', and as this was no longer the case, the most he was willing to pay was fifty rupees.

The assembled people now took sides; some maintaining that the sum demanded was too great, while others as vigorously maintained that the sum offered was too small. Eventually, after giving due consideration to the arguments for and against—arguments that went into very minute and very personal details, and to which Tilni listened with an amused smile on her pretty face—Anderson fixed the price of Tilni at seventy-five rupees, and this sum Kalu was ordered to pay Chadi. Opening his waistband, Kalu produced a string purse, and emptied it on the carpet at Anderson's feet. The contents amounted to fifty-two silver rupees. When two of Kalu's friends had come to his assistance and added another twenty-three rupees, Chadi was told to count the money. When he had done so and stated that the sum was correct, a woman whom I had noticed coming very slowly and apparently very painfully from the direction of the village after all the others were seated and who had sat down a little apart from the rest, got with some difficulty to her feet and said, 'What about me, Your Honour?' 'Who are you?' asked Anderson. 'I am Kalu's wife', she replied.

She was a tall, gaunt woman, every drop of blood drained from her ivory-white face, her body-line distorted with an enormous spleen and her feet swollen—the result of malaria, the scourge of the Terai.

In a tired, toneless voice the woman said that now that Kalu had purchased another wife, she would be homeless, and as she had no relatives in the village, and was too ill to work, she would die of neglect and starvation. Then she covered her face with her sari and began to cry silently, great sobs shaking her wasted frame and tears splashing down on her distorted body.

Here was an unexpected and an unfortunate complication, and one that was for Anderson difficult of solution, for while the case had been under discussion there had been no hint that Kalu already had a wife.

The uncomfortable silence following the woman's pitiful outburst had lasted some time, when Tilni, who had remained standing, ran across to the poor weeping woman, and flinging her strong young arms round her, said, 'Don't cry, sister, don't cry; and don't say you are homeless, for I will share the new hut Kalu has built for me with you, and I will take care of you and nurse you and one half of all that Kalu gives me, I will give you. So don't cry any more, sister, and now come with me and I will take you to our hut.'

As Tilni and the sick woman moved off, Anderson stood up and, blowing his nose violently, said the wind coming down from the hills had given him a damned cold, and that the proceedings were closed for the day. The wind coming down from the hills appeared to have affected others in the same way as it had affected Anderson, for his was not the only nose that was in urgent need of blowing. But the proceedings were not quite over, for Chadi now approached Anderson and asked for the return of his petition. Having torn his petition into small bits, Chadi took the piece of cloth in which he had tied up the seventy-five rupees from his pocket, opened it and said: 'Kalu and I be men of the same village, and as he has now two mouths to feed, one of which requires special food, he will need all his money. So permit me, Your Honour, to return this money to him.'

While touring his domain, Anderson and his predecessors

in pre-red-tape days, settled to the mutual satisfaction of all concerned hundreds, nay thousands, of cases similar to these, without the contestants being put to one pice of expense. Now, since the introduction of red tape, these cases are taken to courts of law where both the complainant and the defendant are bled white, and where seeds of dissension are sown that inevitably lead to more and more court cases, to the enrichment of the legal profession and the ruin of the poor, simple, honest, hardworking peasantry.

5

The Law of the Jungles

Harkwar and Kunthi were married before their total ages had reached double figures. This was quite normal in the India of those days, and would possibly still have been so, had Mahatma Gandhi and Miss Mayo never lived.

Harkwar and Kunthi lived in villages a few miles apart at the foot of the great Dunagiri Mountain, and had never seen each other until the great day when, dressed in bright new clothes, they had, for all too short a time, been the centre of attraction of a vast crowd of relatives and friends. That day lived long in their memories as the wonderful occasion when they had been able to fill their small bellies to bursting- point with halwa and puris. The day also lived for long years in the memory of their respective fathers, for on it, the village bania, who was their 'father and mother', realizing their great necessity, had provided the few rupees that had enabled them to retain the respect of their community by marrying their children at the age that which children should be married, and on the propitious date selected by the priest of the village—and had made a fresh entry against their names in his register.

True, the 50 per cent interest demanded for the accommodation was excessive, but, God willing, a part of it would be paid, for there were other children yet to be married, and who but the good bania was there to help them? Kunthi returned to her father's home after her wedding and for the next few years performed all the duties that children are called upon to perform in the homes of the very poor. The only difference her married state made in her life was that she was no longer permitted to wear the one- piece dress that unmarried girls wear. Her new costume now consisted of three pieces, a chaddar, a yard-and-a-half long, one end of which was tucked into her skirt and the other draped over her head, a tiny sleeveless bodice and a skirt a few inches long.

Several uneventful and carefree years went by for Kunthi until the day came when she was judged old enough to join her husband. Once again the bania came to the rescue and, arrayed in her new clothes, a very tearful girl-bride set out for the home of her boy-husband. The change from one home to another only meant for Kunthi, the performing of chores for her mother-in-law which she had previously performed for her mother. There are no drones in a poor man's household in India; young and old have their allotted work to do and they do it cheerfully. Kunthi was now old enough to help with the cooking, and as soon as the morning meal had been eaten, all who were capable of working for wages set out to perform their respective tasks, which, no matter how minor they were, brought grist to the family mill. Harkwar's father was a mason and was engaged on building a chapel at the American Mission School. It was Harkwar's ambition to follow in his father's profession and, until he had the strength to do so, he helped the family exchequer by carrying the materials used by his father and the other masons, earning two annas a day for his ten hours' labour.

The crops on the low irrigated lands were ripening, and

after Kunthi had washed and polished the metal pots and pans used for the morning meal, she accompanied her mother-in- law and her numerous sisters-in-law to the fields of the headman of the village, where with other women and girls she laboured as many hours as her husband, for half the wage he received. When the day's work was done, the family walked back in the twilight to the hut Harkwar's father had been permitted to build on the headman's land, and with the dry sticks the younger children had collected during their elders' absence, the evening meal was cooked and eaten. Except for the fire, there had never been any other form of illumination in the hut, and when the pots and pans had been cleaned and put away, each member of the family retired to his or her allotted place, Harkwar and his brothers, sleeping with their father, and Kunthi sleeping with the other female members of the family.

When Harkwar was eighteen and Kunthi sixteen, they left, and, carrying their few possessions, set up home in a hut placed at their disposal by an uncle of Harkwar's, in a village three miles from the cantonment of Ranikhet. A number of barracks were under construction in the cantonment and Harkwar had no difficulty in finding work as a mason, nor had Kunthi any difficulty in finding work as a labourer, carrying stones from a quarry to the site of the building.

For four years, the young couple worked on the barracks at Ranikhet, and during this period Kunthi had two children. In November of the fourth year, the buildings were completed and Harkwar and Kunthi had to find new work, for their savings were small and would only keep them in food for a few days.

Winter set in early that year and promised to be unusually severe. The family had no warm clothes, and after a week's unsuccessful search for work, Harkwar suggested that they should migrate to the foothills where he heard a canal headworks was being constructed.

So, early in December, the family set out in high spirits on their long walk to the foothills. The distance between the village in which they had made their home for four years and the canal headworks at Kaladhungi, where they hoped to procure work, was roughly fifty miles.

Sleeping under trees at night, toiling up and down steep and rough roads during the day, and carrying all their worldly possessions and the children by turns, Harkwar and Kunthi, tired and footsore, accomplished the journey to Kaladhungi in six days.

Other landless members of the depressed class had migrated earlier in the winter from the high hills to the foothills and built themselves communal huts capable of housing as many as thirty families. In these huts, Harkwar and Kunthi were unable to find accommodation, so they had to build a hut for themselves. They chose a site at the edge of the forest where there was an abundant supply of fuel, within easy reach of the bazaar, and laboured early and late on a small hut of branches and leaves, for their supply of hard cash had dwindled to a few rupees and there was no friendly bania here to whom they could turn for help.

The forest at the edge of which Harkwar and Kunthi built their hut was a favourite hunting-ground of mine. I had first entered it carrying my old muzzle-loader to shoot red jungle fowl and peafowl for the family larder, and later I had penetrated to every corner, armed with a modern rifle, in search of big game. At the time Harkwar and Kunthi and their two children, Punwa, a boy aged three, and Putali, a girl aged two, took up their residence in the hut, there were in that forest, to my certain knowledge, five tigers, eight leopards, a family of four sloth bears, two Himalayan black bears who had come down from the high hills to feed on wild plums and honey, a number of hyenas who had their burrows in the grasslands five miles away and who visited the forest nightly to feed on the discarded portions of the tigers' and leopards' kills, a pair of wild dogs, numerous jackals and foxes and pine martens, and a variety of civet and other cats.

There were also two pythons, many kinds of snakes, crested and tawny eagles and hundreds of vultures in the forest. I have not mentioned animals such as deer, antelope, pigs, and monkeys, which are harmless to human beings, for they have no part in my story.

The day after the flimsy hut was completed, Harkwar found work as a qualified mason on a daily wage of eight annas with the contractor who was building the canal headworks, and Kunthi purchased for two rupees, a permit from the Forest Department which entitled her to cut grass on the foothills, which she sold as fodder for the cattle of the shopkeepers in the bazaar. For her bundle of green grass weighing anything up to eighty pounds and which necessitated a walk of from ten to fourteen miles, mostly up and down steep hills, Kunthi received four annas, one anna of which was taken by the man who held the Government contract for sale of grass in the bazaar. On the eight annas earned by Harkwar, plus the three annas earned by Kunthi, the family of four lived in comparative comfort, for food was plentiful and cheap and for the first time in their lives they were able to afford one meat meal a month.

Two of the three months that Harkwar and Kunthi intended spending in Kaladhungi, passed very peacefully.

The hours of work were long, and admitted of no relaxation, but to that they had been accustomed from childhood. The weather was perfect, the children kept in good health, and except during the first few days while the hut was being built, they had never gone hungry.

The children had in the beginning been an anxiety, for they were too young to accompany Harkwar to the canal headworks, or Kunthi on her long journeys in search of grass. Then a kindly old crippled woman living in the communal hut a few hundred yards away, came to the rescue by offering to keep a general eye on the children while the parents were away at work. This arrangement worked satisfactorily for two months, and each evening when Harkwar returned from the canal headworks four miles away, and Kunthi returned a little later after selling her grass in the bazaar, they found Punwa and Putali eagerly awaiting their return.

Friday was fair day in Kaladhungi and on that day everyone in the surrounding villages made it a point to visit the bazaar, where open booths were erected for the display of cheap food, fruit and vegetables. On these fair days, Harkwar and Kunthi returned from work half an hour before their usual time, for if any vegetables had been left over, it was possible to buy them at a reduced price before the booths closed down for the night.

One particular Friday, when Harkwar and Kunthi returned to the hut after making their modest purchases of vegetables and a pound of goat's meat, Punwa and Putali were not at the hut to welcome them. On making inquiries from the crippled woman at the communal hut, they learned that she had not seen the children since midday. The woman suggested that they had probably gone to the bazaar to see a merry-go-round that had attracted all the children from the communal hut, and as this seemed a reasonable explanation, Harkwar set off to search the bazaar while Kunthi returned to the hut to prepare the evening meal. An hour later, Harkwar returned with several men who had assisted him in his search to report that no trace of the children could be found, and that of all the people he had questioned, none admitted having seen them.

At that time a rumour was running through the length and breadth of India of the kidnapping of Hindu children by fakirs, for sale on the north-west frontier for immoral purposes. What truth there was in this rumour I am unable to say, but I had frequently read in the daily press of fakirs being manhandled, and on several occasions being rescued by the police from crowds intent on lynching them. It is safe to say that every parent in India had heard these rumours, and when Harkwar and the friends who had helped him in his search, returned to the hut, they communicated their fears to Kunthi that the children had been kidnapped by fakirs, who had probably come to the fair for that purpose.

At the lower end of the village there was a police station in charge of a head constable and two constables. To this police station Harkwar and Kunthi repaired, with a growing crowd of well-wishers. The head constable was a kindly old man who had children of his own, and after he had listened sympathetically to the distracted parents' story, and recorded their statements in his diary, he said that nothing could be done that night, but that next morning he would send the town crier round to all the fifteen villages in Kaladhungi to announce the loss of the children. He then suggested that if the town crier could announce a reward of fifty rupees, it would greatly assist in the safe return of the children. Fifty rupees! Harkwar and Kunthi were aghast at the suggestion, for they did not know there was so much money in all the world. However when the town crier set out on his round the following morning, he was able to announce the reward, for a man in Kaladhungi who had heard of the head constable's suggestion, had offered the money.

The evening meal was eaten late that night. The childrens' portion was laid aside, and throughout the night, a small fire was kept burning, for it was bitterly cold, and at short intervals Harkwar and Kunthi went out into the night to call to their children, though they knew there was no hope of receiving an answer.

At Kaladhungi, two roads cross each other at right angles, one running along the foot of the hills from Haldwani to Ramnagar, and the other running from Nainital to Bazpur. During that Friday night, sitting close to the small fire to keep themselves warm, Harkwar and Kunthi decided that if the children did not turn up by morning, they would go along the former road and make inquiries, as this was the most likely route for the kidnappers to have taken.

At daybreak on Saturday morning, they went to the police station to tell the head constable of their decision, and were instructed to lodge a report at the Haldwani and Ramnagar police stations. They were greatly heartened when the head constable told them that he was sending a letter by mail runner to no less a person than the Inspector of Police at Haldwani, requesting him to telegraph to all railway junctions to keep a look-out for the children, a description of whom he was sending with his letter.

Near sunset that evening, Kunthi returned from her twenty- eight-mile walk to Haldwani and went straight to the police station to inquire about her children and to tell the head constable that, though her quest had been fruitless, she had lodged a report as instructed at the Haldwani police station. Shortly afterwards Harkwar returned from his thirty-six-mile walk to Ramnagar, and he too went straight to the police station to make inquiries and to report that he had found no trace of the children, but had carried out the head constable's instructions. Many friends, including a number of mothers who feared for the safety of their own children, were waiting at the hut to express their sympathy for Harkwar and for Punwa's mother—for, as is the custom in India, Kunthi when she married, lost the name she had been given at birth, and until Punwa was born had been addressed and referred to as 'Harkwar's wife', and after Punwa's birth, as 'Punwa's mother.'

Sunday was a repetition of Saturday, with the difference that instead of going east and west, Kunthi went north to Nainital while Harkwar went south to Bazpur. The former covered thirty miles, and the latter, thirty-two. Starting early and returning at nightfall, the distracted parents traversed many miles of rough roads through dense forests, where people do not usually go except in large parties, and where Harkwar and Kunthi would not have dreamed of going alone had not anxiety for their children overcome their fear of dacoits and of wild animals.

On that Sunday evening, weary and hungry, they returned to their hut from their fruitless visit to Nainital and to Bazpur, to be met by the news that the town crier's visit to the villages and the police inquiries had failed to find any trace of the children. Then they lost heart and gave up all hope of ever seeing Punwa and Putali again. The anger of the gods, that had resulted in a fakir being able to steal their children in broad daylight, was not to be explained.

Before starting on their long walk from the hills, they had consulted the village priest, and he had selected the propitious day for them to set out on their journey. At every shrine they had passed, they had made the requisite offering; at one place, a dry bit of wood, in another a small strip of cloth torn from the hem of Kunthi's chaddar, and in yet another a pice, which they could ill afford. And here, at Kaladhungi, every time they passed the temple that their low caste did not permit them to enter; they had never failed to raise their clasped hands in supplication. Why then had this great misfortune befallen them, who had done all that the gods demanded of them and who had never wronged any man?

Monday found the pair too dispirited and too tired to leave their hut. There was no food, and would be none until they resumed work. But of what use was it to work now, when the children for whom they had ungrudgingly laboured from morn to night, were gone? So, while friends came and went, offering what sympathy they could, Harkwar sat at the door of the hut staring into a bleak and hopeless future, while Kunthi, her tears all gone, sat in a corner, hour after hour, rocking herself to and fro, to and fro.

On that Monday, a man of my acquaintance was herding buffaloes in the jungle in which lived the wild animals and birds I have mentioned. He was a simple soul who had spent the greater part of his life in the jungles herding the buffaloes of the headman at Patabpur village. He knew the danger from tigers, and near sundown he collected the buffaloes and started to drive them to the village, along a cattle track, that ran through the densest part of the jungle. Presently he noticed that as each buffalo got to a certain spot in the track it turned its head to the right and stopped, until urged on by the horns of the animal following. When he got to this spot he also turned his head to the right, and in a little depression a few feet from the track, saw two small children lying.

This man had been in the jungle with his buffaloes when the town crier had made his round of the villages on Saturday, but that night, and the following night also, the kidnapping of Harkwar's children had been the topic of conversation round the village fire, as in fact it had been round every village fire in the whole of Kaladhungi. Here then were the missing children for whom a reward of fifty rupees had been offered. But why had they been murdered and brought to this remote spot? The children were naked, and were clasped in each other's arms. The herdsman defended into the depression and squatted down on his hunkers to determine, if he could, how the children had met their death. That the children were dead he was convinced, yet now as he sat closely scrutinizing them he suddenly saw that they were breathing; that in fact they were not dead, but sound asleep. He was a father himself, and very gently he touched the children and roused them. To touch them was a crime against his caste, for he was a Brahmin and they were low-caste children, but what mattered caste in an emergency like this? So, leaving his buffaloes to find their own way home, he picked up the children, who were too weak to walk, and set out for the Kaladhungi bazaar with one on each shoulder. The man was not too strong himself, for like all who live in the foothills he had suffered much from malaria.

The children were an awkward load and had to be held in position. Moreover, as all the cattle tracks and game paths in this jungle run from north to south, and his way lay from east to west, he had to make frequent detours to avoid impenetrable thickets and deep ravines. But he carried on manfully, resting every now and then in the course of his six- mile walk. Putali was beyond speech, but Punwa was able to talk a little and all the explanation he could give for their being in the jungle was that they had been playing and had got lost.

Harkwar was sitting at the door of his hut staring into the darkening night, in which points of light were beginning to appear as a lantern or cooking-fire was lit here and there, when he saw a small crowd of people appearing from the direction of the bazaar. At the head of the procession, a man was walking, carrying something on his shoulders. From all sides people were converging on the procession and he could hear an excited murmur of 'Harkwar's children'. Harkwar's children. He could not believe his ears, and yet there appeared to be no mistake, for the procession was coming straight towards his hut.

Kunthi, having reached the limit of her misery and of her physical endurance, had fallen asleep curled up in a corner of the hut. Harkwar shook her awake and got her to the door just as the herdsman carrying Punwa and Putali reached it. When the tearful greetings, and blessings and thanks for the rescuer, and the congratulations of friends had partly subsided, the question of the reward the herdsman had earned was mooted. To a poor man, fifty rupees was wealth untold, and with it, the herdsman could buy three buffaloes or ten cows, and be independent for life. But the rescuer was a better man than the crowd gave him credit for. The blessings and thanks that had been showered on his head that night, he said, was reward enough for him, and he stoutly refused to touch one pice of the fifty rupees. Nor would Harkwar or Kunthi accept the reward either as a gift or a loan. They had got back the children they had lost all hope of ever seeing again, and would resume work as their strength returned. In the meantime, the milk and sweets and puris that one and another of the assembled people, out of the goodness of their hearts, had run to the bazaar to fetch would be amply sufficient to sustain them.

Two-year-old Putali and three-year-old Punwa were lost at midday on Friday, and were found by the herdsman at about 5 p.m. on Monday, a matter of seventy-seven hours. I have given a description of the wildlife which, to my knowledge, was in the forest in which the children spent those seventy-seven hours, and it would be unreasonable to assume that none of the animals or birds saw, heard, or smelt the children. And yet, when the herdsman put Putali and Punwa into their parents' arms, there was not a single mark of tooth or claw on them.

I once saw a tigress stalking a month-old kid. The ground was very open and the kid saw the tigress while she was still some distance away and started bleating, where on the tigress gave up her stalk and walked straight up to it. When the tigress had approached to within a few yards, the kid went forward to meet her, and on reaching the tigress stretched out its neck and put up its head to smell her. For the duration of a few heartbeats, the month-old kid and the Queen of the Forest stood nose to nose, and then the queen turned and walked off in the direction from which she had come.

When Hitler's war was nearing its end, in one week I read extracts from speeches of three of the greatest men in the British Empire, condemning war atrocities, and accusing the enemy of attempting to introduce the 'law of the jungle' into the dealings of warring man and man. Had the Creator made the same law for man as He has made for the jungle folk, there would be no wars, for the strong in man would have the same consideration for the weak as is the established law of the jungles.

6

The Brothers

The long years of training boys for jungle warfare were over, and we were sitting one morning after breakfast on the veranda of our cottage at Kaladhungi. My sister Maggie was knitting a khaki pullover for me, and I was putting the finishing touches to a favourite fly-rod that suffered from years of disuse, when a man wearing a clean but much- patched cotton suit walked up the steps of the veranda with a broad grin on his face, salaamed, and asked if we remembered him.

Many people, clean and not so clean, old and young, rich and poor (but mostly poor), Hindus, Mohammedans and Christians, walked up those steps, for our cottage was at a crossroads at the foot of the hills and on the borderline between the cultivated land and the forest. All who were sick or sorry, in want of a helping hand, or in need of a little human companionship and a cup of tea, whether living on the cultivated land or working in the forest or just passing on their way from one place to another, found their way to our cottage. Had a record been maintained over the years of only the sick and injured treated, it would have had thousands of names in it. And the cases dealt with would have covered every ailment that human flesh is heir to—and subject to, when living in an unhealthy area, working in forests on dangerous jobs among animals who occasionally lose their tempers.

There was the case of the woman who came one morning and complained that her son had great difficulty in eating the linseed poultice that had been given to her the previous evening to apply on a boil (as the poultice did not appear to have done the boy any good, she asked to have the medicine changed). And the case of the old Mohammedan woman who came late one evening, with tears streaming down her face, and begged Maggie to save her husband who was dying of pneumonia. She looked a glance at the tablets of M. & B. 693 and asked if that was all that was to be given to a dying man to make him well; but next day she returned with a beaming countenance to report that her husband had recovered, and begged for the same kind of medicine for the four friends she had brought with her, each of whom had husbands as old as hers who might at any time get pneumonia. And there was the case of the girl about eight years old, who, after some difficulty in reaching the latch of the gate, marched up to the veranda, firmly holding the hand of a boy some two years younger, and asked for medicine for the boy's sore eyes. She sat herself down on the ground, made the boy lie on his back, and having got his head between her knees said, 'Now, Miss Sahib, you can do anything you like to him.' This girl was the daughter of the headman of a village six miles away. Seeing her classmate suffering from sore eyes, she had taken it upon herself to bring him to Maggie for treatment, and for a whole week, until his eyes were quite well, the young samaritan brought the boy to the cottage, though in order to do so she had to walk an additional four miles each day.

Then there was the case of the sawyer from Delhi, who limped into the compound one day with his right leg ripped open by the tusk of a pig, from his heel to the back of his knee. All the time his leg was being attended to, he swore at the unclean beast that had done this terrible thing to him, for he was a follower of the Prophet. His story was that when that morning he had approached the tree he had felled the previous day, to saw it up, a pig which had been sheltering among the branches ran against him and cut his leg. When I suggested that it was his own fault for having got in the way of the pig, he indignantly exclaimed: 'With the whole jungle to run about in, what need was there for it to have run against me when I had done nothing to offend it, and in fact before I had even seen it?'

There was another sawyer too. While turning over a log, he had been stung on the palm of his hand by a scorpion 'as big as this'. After treatment, he rolled on the ground loudly lamenting his fate and asserting that the medicine was doing him no good, but not long after he was observed to be holding his sides and choking with laughter. It was the day of the children's annual fete, and when the races had been run and the two hundred children and their mothers had been fed on sweets and fruit, a circle had been formed. A blindfolded boy had been set to break a paper bag containing nuts of all kinds, which was slung between two bamboos held upright by two men, and it was when the boy brought his stick down on the head of one of these men that the scorpion-patient was found to be laughing the loudest of all the assembly. When asked how the pain now was, the man replied that it had gone, and that in any case he would not mind how many scorpions stung him provided he could take part in a tamasha like this.

The members of our family have been amateur physicians for more years than I can remember, and as Indians, especially the poorer ones, have long memories, and never forget a kindness no matter how trivial it may have been, not all the people who walked up the steps of our cottage at Kaladhungi were patients. Many there were those who had marched for days over rough tracks in all weathers to thank us for small kindnesses shown to them, maybe the previous year, or maybe many years previously.

One of these was a sixteen-year-old boy, who with his mother had been housed for some days in our village while Maggie treated his mother for influenza and badly inflamed eyes; now he had done a march of many days to bring Maggie his mother's thanks and a present of a few pomegranates which his mother had picked for her 'with her own hand'. And only that day, an hour before the man wearing the patched suit had arrived, an old man had walked up the steps and seated himself on the veranda with his back to one of the pillars and, after looking at me for some time, had shaken his head in a disapproving manner and said, 'You are looking much older, Sahib, than you were when I last saw you.' 'Yes', I replied, 'all of us are apt to look older after ten years.' 'Not all of us, Sahib,' he rejoined, 'for I look and feel no older than when I last sat in your veranda not ten, but twelve years ago. On that occasion I was returning on foot from a pilgrimage to Badrinath, and seeing your gate open, and being tired and in urgent need of ten rupees, I asked you to let me rest for a while, and appealed to you for help. I am now returning from another pilgrimage, this time to the sacred city of Benares. I am in no need of money and have only come to thank you for the help you gave me before and to tell you that I got home safely. After this smoke, and a little rest, I shall return to rejoin my family, whom I left at Haldwani.' A fourteen-mile walk each way. And in spite of his assertion that twelve years had not made him look or feel any older, he was a frail old man.

Though the face of the man in the patched cotton suit, who now stood before us on the veranda, was vaguely familiar, we could not remember his name or the circumstances in which we had last seen him. Seeing that he was not recognized, the man removed his coat, opened his shirt, and exposed his chest and right shoulder. That shoulder brought him to instant memory. He was Narwa, the basket-maker, and there was some excuse for our not having recognized him, for when we had last seen him, six years previously, he was mere skin and bone; only with great difficulty had he been able to put one foot before another, and he had needed a stick to support himself. Looking now at his misshapen shoulder, the crushed and broken bones of which had calloused without being set, the puckered and discoloured skin of his chest and back, and his partially withered right arm, we, who for three months, had watched his gallant fight for life, marvelled how well he had survived his ordeal. Moving his arm up and down, and closing and opening his hand, Narwa said that his arm was getting stronger every day. His fingers had not got stiff, as we feared they would, so he had been able to resume his trade. His object now, he said, was to show us that he was quite well and to thank Maggie—which he proceeded to do by putting his head on her feet—for having supplied all his wants, and the wants of his wife and child, during the months he had lain between life and death.

Narwa and Haria were not blood brothers, though they so described themselves. They had been born and had grown up in the same village near Almora, and when old enough to work, had adopted the same profession, basket-making—

which means that they were untouchables, for in the United Provinces, baskets are only made by untouchables.

During the summer months, Narwa and Haria worked at their trade in their village near Almora, and in the winter months they came down to Kaladhungi where there was a great demand for the huge baskets, measuring up to fifteen feet in diameter, which they made for our villagers for the storage of grain. In their hill village near Almora, they made their baskets of ringals—thin bamboo, an inch thick and upto twenty feet long, which grows at an altitude of four to ten thousand feet, and which incidentally makes the most perfect of fly-rods—and in Kaladhungi they made them of bamboos.

The bamboos in Kaladhungi grow in the Government Reserved Forests, and we who cultivate land near the Reserved Forests are permitted to cut a certain number each year for our personal use. But people who use the bamboos for commercial purposes have to take out a licence from the forest guard of the area, paying two annas per headload, and a small consideration to the forest guard for his trouble in filling in the licence. As the licence is a personal one and covers an individual headload, it is safe to assume that as many lengths of two-year-old bamboos—the age when a bamboo is best for basket-making—were included in the load as a man could carry.

At daybreak on the morning of 26 December 1939, Narwa and Haria set out from their communal hut near the bazaar at Kaladhungi to walk eight miles to Nalni village, obtain a licence from the forest guard, cut two headloads of bamboos in the Nalni Reserved Forests, and return to Kaladhungi the same evening. It was bitterly cold when they started, so the two men wrapped coarse cotton sheets round their shoulders to keep out the cold. For a mile, their way ran along the canal bank. Then, after negotiating the series of high walls which form the headworks of the canal, they took a footpath which runs alternately through patches of dense scrub jungle and over long stretches of the boulder-strewn bank of the Boar river, stretches where a pair of otters are usually to be seen in the early morning, and where, when the sun is on the water, mahseer upto three or four pounds can be taken on a fly-rod. Two miles up, they crossed by a shallow ford from the right to the left bank of the river and entered a tree and grass jungle, where morning and evening are to be seen several small herds of chital and sambhar, and an occasional kakar, leopard, or tiger. A mile through this jungle, they came to where the hills converge, and where some years previously, Robin picked up the tracks of the Bachelor of Powalgarh. From this point onwards, the valley opens out and is known to all who graze cattle, or who poach or shoot in the area, as Samal Chour. In this valley one has to walk warily, for the footpath is used almost as much by tigers as it is by human beings.

At the upper end of the valley, the footpath, before going steeply up the hill for two miles to Nalni village, passes through a strip of grass. This strip of eight-foot grass is thirty yards wide and extends for about fifty yards on either side of the path. In anticipation of the stiff climb up the Nalni hill, shortly before reaching the grass, Narwa divested himself of his cotton sheet, folded it small and placed it on his right shoulder. Haria was leading, with Narwa following a few steps behind, and he had only gone three or four yards into the grass when he heard the angry roar of a tiger, and simultaneously a shriek from Narwa. Haria turned and dashed back, and on the open ground at the edge of the grass, he saw Narwa on his back with a tiger lying diagonally across him. Narwa's feet were nearest to him, and grasping an ankle in each hand, he started to pull him away from under the tiger. As he did this the tiger stood up, turned towards him and started to growl. After dragging Narwa along on his back for a short distance Haria got his arms round him and set him on his feet. But Narwa was too badly injured and shaken to stand or walk, so Haria put his arms round him, and alternately dragged and carried him—while the tiger continued to growl—through the open ground skirting the grass, and so regained the path to Nalni village.

By superhuman efforts, Haria eventually got Narwa to Nalni, where it was found that in spite of the folded sheet which he had been carrying on his right shoulder, and which Haria had retrieved while pulling him away, the tiger had crushed the bones of the shoulder, lacerated the flesh, and exposed the bones on the right side of the chest and back. All four of the tiger's canine teeth had penetrated some eight folds of the sheet, and but for this obstruction they would have met in Narwa's chest and inflicted a fatal wound.

The forest guard and the people of Nalni were unable to do anything for Narwa, so Haria hired a pack pony for two rupees, mounted Narwa on it, and set out for Kaladhungi. The distance, as I have already said, was eight miles, but Haria was unwilling to face the tiger a second time so he made a wide detour through Musabanga village, adding ten miles to Narwa's agonizing journey. There were no saddles at Nalni and he had been mounted on a hard pack used for carrying grain, and the first nine miles of his ride was over incredibly steep and rough ground.

Maggie was having tea on the veranda of our cottage when Narwa, soaked in blood and being held on the pony by Haria, arrived at the steps. A glance was enough to show that the case was one she could not deal with, so she quickly gave Narwa a stiff dose of sal volatile—for he was on the point of fainting—and made a sling for his arm. Then she tore up a bed sheet to be used for bandages and wrote a note to the Assistant Surgeon in charge of the Kaladhungi hospital, begging him to attend to Narwa immediately, and do all he could for him. She gave the note to our head boy and sent him to the hospital with the two men.

I was out bird shooting that day with a party of friends who were spending their Christmas holiday at Kaladhungi, and when I returned in the late evening, Maggie told me about Narwa. Early next morning I was at the hospital, where I was informed by a very young and very inexperienced doctor that he had done all he could for Narwa, but as he had little hope of his recovery, and no arrangements for in-patients, he had sent Narwa home after treating him.

In the large communal hut, which housed about twenty families, each of which appeared to have a record number of small children, I found Narwa lying in a corner on a bed of straw and leaves. It was the last place for a man in his terrible condition to be in, for his wounds were showing signs of getting septic. For a week Narwa lay in the corner of the noisy and insanitary hut, at times raving in high fever, at times in a state of coma, watched over by his weeping wife, and his devoted 'brother' Haria, and other friends.

It was now apparent, even to my inexperienced eyes, that if Narwa's septic wounds were not opened up, drained, and cleaned, there was a certainty of the doctor's predictions being fulfilled, so, after making arrangements for his care while under treatment, I removed him to the hospital. To give the young doctor credit, when he undertook to do the job, he did it thoroughly, and many of the long scars on his chest and back that Narwa will carry to the burning-ghat, were made not by the tiger but by the doctor's lancet, which he used very freely.

With the exception of professional beggars, the poor in India can only eat when they work, and as Narwa's wife's days were fully occupied in visiting him at the hospital, and later in nursing him when he returned to the communal hut, and in caring for her three-year-old girl and her young baby, Maggie supplied all Narwa's wants, and the wants of his family (Small hospitals in India do not provide either attendants or food for patients). Three months later, reduced to skin and bone and with a right arm that looked as though it could never be used again, Narwa crawled from the hut to our cottage to bid us goodbye and the next day he and Haria and their families set out for their village near Almora.

After visiting Narwa in the communal hut that first morning, and getting a firsthand account of the incident from Haria, I was convinced that the tiger's encounter with Narwa was accidental. However, to satisfy myself that my reconstruction of the event was right—and to shoot the tiger if I was wrong—I followed, foot by foot, the track the brothers had taken the previous day when on their way to Nalni village. For a few yards the track runs along the edge of the strip of high grass at the foot of the Nalni hill, before turning at right angles to cross the grass. Shortly before the two men arrived at this spot, the tiger had killed a sambhar stag and carried it into the grass close to the right-hand side of the track. When Haria entered the grass, the tiger heard the rustling, and coming out, ran into Narwa, who was a few yards behind Haria and a yard or two from the turning. The encounter was accidental, for the grass was too thick and too high for the tiger to have seen Narwa before he bumped into him. Furthermore, it had made no attempt to savage Narwa, and had even allowed Haria to drag the man on whom it was lying, away from under it. So the tiger was allowed to live, and was later induced to join the party of tigers that are mentioned in the chapter 'Just Tigers' in *Man-eaters of Kumaon.*

Of all the brave deeds that I have witnessed, or that I have read or heard about, I count Haria's rescue of Narwa the greatest. Unarmed and alone in a great expanse of jungle, to respond to the cry of a companion in distress and to pull that companion away from an angry tiger that was lying on him, and then to drag and carry that companion for two miles up a steep hill to a place of safety, not knowing but that the tiger was following, needed a degree of courage that is given to few, and that any man could envy. When I took down Haria's statement—which was later corroborated in every detail by Narwa—with the object, unknown to him, of his act receiving recognition, so far from thinking that he had done anything deserving of commendation, after I had finished questioning him he said: 'I have not done anything, Sahib, have I, that is likely to bring trouble on me or on my brother Narwa?'

And Narwa, a few days later, when I took down what I feared would be his dying declaration, said in a voice racked with pain and little above a whisper, 'Don't let my brother get into any trouble, Sahib, for it was not his fault that the tiger attacked me, and he risked his life to save mine'.

I should have liked to have been able to end my story by telling you that Haria's brave act, and Narwa's heroic fight for life against great odds, had been acknowledged by a certificate of merit, or some other small token of award, for both were poor men. Unfortunately, red tape proved too much for me, for the Government was not willing to make any award in a case of which the truth could not be sworn to by independent and unbiased witnesses.

So one of the bravest deeds ever performed has gone unrecognized because there were no 'independent and unbiased witnesses'; and of the brothers, Haria is the poorer of the two, for he has nothing to show for the part he played, while Narwa has his scars and the sheet with many holes, stained with his blood.

For many days I toyed with the idea of appealing to His Majesty the King, but with a World War starting and all it implied, I very reluctantly abandoned the idea.

7

Sultana: India's Robin Hood

In a country as vast as India, with its great areas of forest land and bad communications, and with its teeming population chronically on the verge of starvation, it is easy to understand the temptations to embark on a life of crime, and the difficulty the Government have in rounding up criminals. In addition to the ordinary criminals to be found in all countries, there are in India whole tribes classed as criminals who are segregated in settlements set apart for them by the Government and subjected to a greater or lesser degree of restraint according to the crimes they specialize in.

While I was engaged on welfare work during a part of the last war, I frequently visited one of these criminal settlements. The inmates were not kept under close restraint, and I had many interesting talks with them and with the Government representative in charge of the settlement. In an effort to wean this tribe from a life of crime, the Government had given them, free of rent, a large tract of alluvial land on the left bank of the Jumna river in the Meerut District. This rich land produced bumper crops of sugarcane, wheat, barley, rape seed and other cereals, but crime persisted. The Government representative blamed the girls, who, he said, refused to marry any but successful criminals. The tribe specialized in robbery, and there were old men in the settlement who trained the younger generation on a profit- sharing basis.

Men were allowed to leave the settlement on ticket of leave for stated periods, but women were not permitted to leave. The elders of the tribe strictly enforced three rules: first, that all robberies were to be carried out single-handed; second, that the scene of the crime was to be as distant from the settlement as possible; and third, that violence, while committing the crime, was not to be resorted to in any circumstances.

The method invariably adopted by a young man, after he had completed his training, was to secure employment as a house servant with a rich man in Calcutta, Bombay, or some other distant city, and when opportunity offered, to rob his master of articles which could be easily secreted, such as gold, jewellery, or precious stones. On one occasion while I was paying a number of young men who had been driving black partridge out of a sugarcane field for me, the Government representative informed me that the young man into whose hands I had just dropped his wage of eight annas, plus two annas for a runner he had retrieved, had returned to the settlement a few days previously, after an absence of a year, with a diamond worth thirty thousand rupees.

After valuation by the experts of the tribe, the diamond had been hidden, and the most sought-after girl in the settlement had promised to marry the successful criminal during the next marriage season. Another of the men standing near by, who had not taken part in the partridge drive, had conceived the novel plan of impressing the girl of his choice by driving up to the settlement, along a most appalling cart-track, in a new motor car he had stolen in Calcutta. In order to carry out his plan, he had first had to pay for driving lessons.

Some members of criminal tribes who are not subjected to strict control, find employment as night watchmen in private houses, and I know of instances where it was a sufficient guarantee against theft for the watchman to place a pair of his shoes on the door step of the house in which he was employed. This may savour of blackmail, but it was cheap blackmail, for the wages paid, varied from three to five rupees a month, according to the standing of the criminal, and the money was easily earned as all the watchman had to do was to place his shoes in position at night, and remove them again the next morning.

Owing to their preference for violent crime, the Bhantus were one of the criminal tribes in the United Provinces that were kept under strict restraint, and Sultana, the famous dacoit who, for three years, defied all the Government's efforts to capture him, was a member of this tribe. It is about Sultana that this story is written.

When I first knew it, Naya Gaon was one of the most nourishing villages in the Terai and Bhabar—the tract of land running along the foothills of the Himalayas. Every yard of the rich soil, carved out of virgin forest, was under intensive cultivation, and the hundred or more tenants were prosperous, contented and happy. Sir Henry Ramsay, the King of Kumaon, had brought these hardy people down from the Himalayas, and for a generation they retained their vigour and flourished exceedingly.

Malaria at that time was known as 'Bhabar fever', and the few doctors, scattered over a wide area, who were responsible for the health of the people, had neither the ability nor the means to cope with this scourge of the foothills. Naya Gaon, situated in the heart of the forest, was one of the first villages in the Bhabar to be decimated by the disease. Field after field went out of cultivation as the tenants died, until only a handful of the sturdy pioneers were left, and when these survivors were given land in our village, Naya Gaon reverted to jungle.

Only once in later years was an attempt made to recultivate the land, the intrepid pioneer on this occasion being a doctor from Punjab; but when first his daughter, then his wife, and finally he himself died of malaria, Naya Gaon for the second time went back to the jungle.

On the land which had been cleared with great labour, on which bumper crops of sugarcane, wheat, mustard and rice had been grown, luxuriant grass sprang up. Attracted by this rich feed, the cattle from our village three miles away adopted the deserted fields of Naya Gaon as their regular feeding ground. When cattle graze for long periods over open ground surrounded by jungle, they invariably attract carnivora, and I was not surprised to hear one year, on our descent from our summer home in Nainital to our winter home in Kaladhungi, that a leopard had taken up residence in the jungles adjoining the grazing-ground and that he was taking heavy toll of our cattle. There were no trees on the grassland in which I could sit over a kill, so I determined to shoot the leopard either in the early morning, when he was on his way to lie up in thick cover for the day, or in the evening, when he was returning to a kill or intent on making a fresh one. For either of these plans to be effective, it was necessary to discover in what part of the surrounding jungles the leopard had made his home, so early one morning Robin and I set out to glean this information.

Naya Gaon—for though the land has been out of cultivation for many years, it retains its name to this day—is bounded on the north by the road known as the Kandi Sarak, and on the east by the old Trunk Road, which, before the advent of railways, connected the plains of the United Provinces with the interior of Kumaon.

To the south and west, Naya Gaon is bounded by dense jungle. Both the Kandi Sarak and the Trunk Road are little used in these days and I decided to try them first before trying the more difficult ground to the south and west. At the junction of the roads, where in the days gone by, a police guard was posted for the protection of wayfarers against dacoits, Robin and I found the tracks of a female leopard. This leopard was well known to Robin and me, for she had lived for several years in a heavy patch of Iantana at the lower end of our village. Apart from never molesting our cattle, she had kept pigs and monkeys from damaging our crops, so we ignored her tracks and carried on along the Trunk Road in the direction of Garuppu. There had been no traffic on the road since the previous evening, and the tracks of animals who had used or crossed it were registered on the dusty surface.

From the rifle in my hands, Robin, who was a wise dog and my constant companion, knew we were not after birds so he paid no attention to the peafowl that occasionally scurried across the road or to the jungle fowl that were scratching up the dead leaves at the side of it, but concentrated on the tracks of a tigress and her two half-grown cubs that had gone down the road an hour ahead of us. In places, the wide road was overgrown with short dub grass. On this dew-drenched grass the cubs had rolled and tumbled, and Robin filled his nostrils to his heart's content with the sweet and terrifying smell of tigers. The family had kept to the road for a mile and had then gone east along a game track. Three miles from the junction, and two miles above Garuppu, a well-used game track coming from the direction of Naya Gaon crosses the road diagonally, and on this track we saw the fresh pug marks of a big male leopard.

We had found what we were looking for. This leopard had come from the grazing ground and crossed the road. It was capable of killing a full-grown cow and there were not likely to be two leopards of this size in the same area. Robin was keen on following up the tracks, but the dense scrub jungle the leopard was making for—the same jungle in which Kunwar Singh and Har Singh had nearly lost their lives some years previously—was not suitable for stalking an animal with the sight and hearing of a leopard. Moreover, I had a better and simpler plan of making contact with the leopard, so we turned about and made for home and breakfast.

After lunch, Robin and I, accompanied by Maggie, retraced our steps down the Garuppu road. The leopard had not killed any of our cattle the previous day but he might have killed a chital or a pig which shared the grazing ground with the cattle; and even if he had no kill to return to, there was a very good chance of his visiting his regular hunting ground. So Maggie and I, with Robin lying between us, took up position behind a bush on the side of the road, a hundred yards from the game track along which the leopard had gone that morning. We had been in position about an hour, listening to the multitude of bird calls, when a peacock in full plumage majestically crossed the road and went down the game path. A little later, ten or a dozen chital, in the direction of the heavy jungle in which we expected the leopard to be lying up, warned the jungle folk of the presence of a leopard. Ten minutes thereafter, and a little nearer to us, a single chital repeated the warning. The leopard was on the move and coming in our direction, and as he was making no attempt to conceal himself he was probably on his way to a kill.

Robin had lain with chin on outstretched paws without movement, listening as we were, to what the jungle folk had to say, and when he saw me draw up my leg and rest the rifle on my knee, his body, which was against my left leg, started to tremble. The spotted killer, whom he feared more than any other beast in the jungle, would presently put its head out of the bushes and, after looking up and down the road, would come towards us. Whether it died in its tracks, or roared and tumbled about with a mortal wound, he would remain perfectly still and silent, for he was taking part in a game with every move of which he was familiar, and which was as fascinating as it was terrifying.

After going a short distance down the game path, the peacock had climbed into the branches of a plum tree and was busily engaged in eating ripe fruit. Suddenly it sprang into the air with a harsh scream and alighted on the limb of a dead tree, adding its warning to that already given by the chital. A few minutes now, five at the most, for the leopard would approach the road very cautiously, and then out of the corner of my eye I caught sight of a movement far down the road. It was a man running, and every now and then, without slackening his pace, he looked over his shoulder behind him. To see a man on that road at this hour of the evening—the sun was near setting—was very unusual, and to see him alone was even more unusual. Every stride the man took lessened our chances of bagging the leopard. However, that could not be helped, for the runner was evidently in great distress, and possibly in need of help. I recognized him while he was still some distance from us; he was a tenant in a village adjoining ours, who during the winter months, was engaged as herdsman at a cattle station three miles east of Garuppu.

On catching sight of us the runner started violently, but when he recognized me he came towards us and in a very agitated voice said, 'Run, Sahib, run for your life! Sultana's men are after me.'

He was winded and in great distress. Taking no notice of my invitation to sit down and rest, he turned his leg and said, 'see what they have done to me! If they catch me they will surely kill me and you also, if you do not run.' The leg he turned for our inspection was slashed from the back of the knee to the heel, and dust-clotted blood was flowing from the ugly wound. Telling the man that if he would not rest, there was, at least, no need for him to run any more, I moved out of the bushes to where I could get a clear view down the road, while the man limped off in the direction of his village. Neither the leopard nor Sultana's men showed up, and when there was no longer light for accurate shooting, Maggie and I, with a very disgusted Robin at our heels, returned to our home at Kaladhungi.

Next morning I got the man's story. He was grazing his buffaloes between Garuppu and the cattle station, when he heard a gunshot. The nephew of the headman of his village had arrived at the cattle station at dawn that morning with the object of poaching a chital, and while he had been sitting in the shade of a tree, speculating as to whether the shot had been effective or not and, if effective, whether a portion of the venison would be left at the cattle station for his evening meal, he heard a rustle behind him. Looking round, he saw five men standing over him. He was told to get up and take the party to where the gun had been fired.

When he said he had been asleep and had not heard the shot he was ordered to lead the way to the cattle station, to which they thought the gunman would probably go. The party had no firearms, but the man who appeared to be their leader had a naked sword in his hand and said he would cut the herdsman's head off with it if he attempted to run away or shout a warning.

As they made their way through the jungle, the swordsman informed the herdsman that they were members of Sultana's gang and that Sultana was camped near by. When he heard the shot, Sultana had ordered them to bring him the gun. Therefore if they met with any opposition at the cattle station they would burn it down and kill their guide. This threat presented my friend with a dilemma. His companions at the cattle station were a tough lot, and if they offered resistance he would undoubtedly be killed; on the other hand, if they did not resist, his crime in leading the dreaded Sultana's men to the station would never be forgotten or forgiven. While these unpleasant thoughts were running through his head, a chital stag pursued by a pack of wild dogs came dashing through the jungle and passed within a few yards of them. Seeing that his escort had stopped and were watching the chase, the herdsman dived into the high grass on the side of the path and, despite the wound he received on his leg as the swordsman tried to cut him down, he had managed to shake his pursuers off and gain the Trunk Road, where in due course, he ran into us while we were waiting for the leopard.

Sultana was a member of the Bhantu criminal tribe. With the rights and wrongs of classing a tribe as 'criminal' and confining it within the four walls of the Najibabad Fort, I am not concerned. It suffices to say that Sultana, with his young wife and infant son and some hundreds of other Bhantus, was confined in the fort under the charge of the Salvation Army. Chafing at his confinement, he scaled the mud walls of the fort one night and escaped, as any young and high-spirited man would have done. This escape had been effected a year previous to the opening of my story and during that year Sultana had collected a hundred kindred spirits, all armed with guns, around him. This imposing gang, whose declared object was dacoity, led a roving life in the jungles of the Terai and Bhabar, their activities extending from Gonda in the east to Saharanpur in the west, a distance of several hundred miles, with occasional raids into the adjoining province of Punjab.

There are many fat files in Government offices on the activities of Sultana and his gang of dacoits. I have not had access to these files, and if my story, which only deals with events in which I took part or events which came to my personal notice, differs or conflicts in any respect with Government reports, I can only express my regret. At the same time, I do not retract one word of my story.

I first heard of Sultana when he was camping in the Garuppu jungles a few miles from our winter home at Kaladhungi. Percy Wyndham was at that time Commissioner of Kumaon, and as the Terai and Bhabar forests in which Sultana had apparently established himself were in Wyndham's charge, he asked the Government for the services of Freddy Young, a keen young police officer with a few years' service in the United Provinces to his credit. The Government granted Wyndham's request, and sanctioned the creation of a Special Dacoity Police Force of three hundred picked men. Freddy was put in supreme command of this force and given a free hand in the selection of his men. He earned a lot of unpopularity by building up his force with the best men from adjoining districts, for Sultana was a coveted prize and their own officers resented having to surrender men who might have helped them to acquire the prize.

While Freddy was mustering his force, Sultana was getting his hand in by raiding small townships in the Terai and Bhabar. Freddy's first attempt to capture Sultana was made in the forests west of Ramnagar. The Forest Department was felling a portion of these forests, employing a large labour force, and one of the contractors in charge of the labour was induced to invite Sultana, who was known to be camping in the vicinity, to a dance to be followed by a feast. Sultana and his merry men accepted the invitation, but just before the festivities began they prevailed on their host to make a slight alteration in the programme and have the feast first and the dance later. Sultana said his men would enjoy the dance more on full stomachs than on empty ones.

Here it is necessary to interrupt my story to explain for the benefit of those who have never been in the East, that guests at a dance, or a 'nautch' as it is called here, do not take any part in the proceedings. The dancing is confined to a troop of professional dancing-girls and their male orchestra.

Funds in plenty were available on both sides and, as money goes as far in the East towards buying information as it does in the West, one of the first moves of the two contestants in the game that was to be played, was the organization of efficient secret services. Here Sultana had the advantage, for whereas Freddy could only reward for services rendered, Sultana could not only reward but could also punish for information withheld, or for information about his movements to the police, and when his method of dealing with offenders became known, none were willing to court his displeasure.

Having known what it was to be poor, really poor, during his long years of confinement in the Najibabad Fort, Sultana had a warm corner in his heart for all poor people. It was said of him that, throughout his career as a dacoit, he never robbed a pice from a poor man, never refused an appeal for charity, and paid twice the price asked for all he purchased from small shopkeepers. Little wonder then that his intelligence staff numbered hundreds and that he knew the invitation he had received to the dance and feast had been issued at Freddy's instigation.

Meanwhile plans were on foot for the great night. The contractor, reputed to be a rich man, extended invitations to his friends in Ramnagar and in Kashipur; the best dancing-girls and their orchestras were engaged, and large quantities of eatables and drink—the latter specially for the benefit of the dacoits—were purchased and transported by bullock cart to the camp.

At the appointed time on the night that was to see the undoing of Sultana, the contractor's guests assembled and the feast began. It is possible that the contractor's friends did not show who their fellow guests were, for on these occasions the different castes sit in groups by themselves and the illumination provided by firelight and a few lanterns was of the poorest. Sultana and his men ate and drank wisely and well, and when the feast was nearing its end, the dacoit leader led his host aside, thanked him for his hospitality, and said that as he and his men had a long way to go, he regretted they could not stay for the dance. Before leaving, however, he requested—and Sultana's requests were never disregarded—that the festivities should continue as had been arranged.

The principal instrument of music at a nautch is a drum, and the sound of the drums was to be Freddy's signal to leave the position he had taken up and deploy his force to surround the camp. One section of this force was led by a forest guard, and the night being dark, the forest guard lost his way. This section, which was to have blocked Sultana's line of retreat, remained lost for the remainder of the night. As a matter of fact, the forest guard, who had to live in the forest with Sultana and was a wise man, need not have given himself the trouble of getting lost, for by his request for a slight alteration in the programme Sultana had given himself ample time to get clear of the net before the signal was given. So all that the attacking force found when they arrived at the camp, after a long and a difficult march through dense forest, was a troop of frightened girls, their even more frightened orchestra, and the mystified friends of the contractor.

After his escape from the Ramnagar forests Sultana paid a visit to Punjab. Here, with no forests in which to shelter, he was out of his element and after a brief stay, which yielded a hundred thousand rupees' worth of gold ornaments, he returned to the dense jungles of the United Provinces. On his way back from Punjab, he had to cross the Ganges canal, the bridges over which are spaced at intervals of four miles, and as his movements were known, the bridges he was likely to cross were heavily guarded. Avoiding these, Sultana made for a bridge which his intelligence staff informed him was not guarded, and on his way, passed close to a large village in which a band was playing Indian music. On learning from his guides that a rich man's son was being married, he ordered them to take him to the village.

The wedding party and some thousand guests were assembled on a wide open space in the centre of the village. As he entered the glare of the high-powered lamps, Sultana's appearance caused a stir, but he requested the assembly to remain seated and added that if they complied with his request they had nothing to fear. He then summoned the headman of the village and the father of the bridegroom and made it known that, as this was a propitious time for the giving and receiving of gifts, he would like the headman's recently purchased gun for himself and ten thousand rupees in cash for his men. The gun and the money were produced in the shortest time possible, and having wished the assembly good night, Sultana led his men out of the village. Not till the following day did he learn that his lieutenant, Pailwan, had abducted the bride. Sultana did not approve of women being molested by his gang, so Pailwan was severely reprimanded and the girl was sent back, with a suitable present to compensate her for the inconvenience to which she had been put.

After the incident of the herdsman's slashed leg, Sultana remained in our vicinity for some time. He moved camp frequently and I came upon several old sites while out shooting. It was at this time that I had a very exciting experience.

One evening I shot a fine leopard on a fire-track five miles from home, and as there was not sufficient time to collect carriers to bring it in, I skinned it on the spot and carried the skin home; but on arrival I found that I had left my favourite hunting-knife behind.

Early next morning I set out to retrieve the knife and as I approached the spot where I had left it, I saw the glimmer of a fire through a forest glade, some distance from the track. Reports of Sultana's presence in this forest had been coming in for some days, and on the spur of the moment I decided to investigate the fire. Heavy dew on the dead leaves made it possible to move without sound, so taking what cover was available, I stalked the fire, which was burning in a little hollow, and found some twenty to twenty-five men sitting round it. Stacked upright against a nearby tree, the fire glinting on their barrels, were a number of guns. Sultana was not present, for, though I had not seen him up to that time, he had been described to me as a young man, small and trim, who invariably dressed in semi-military khaki uniform. This was evidently part of his gang, however, and what was I going to do about it? The old head constable and his equally elderly force of two constables at Kaladhungi would be of little help, and Haldwani, where there was a big concentration of police, was fifteen miles away.

While I was considering my next move, I heard one of the men say it was time to be going. Fearing that if I now tried to retreat I should be seen, and trouble might follow, I took a few rapid steps forward and got between the men and their guns. As I did so, a ring of surprised faces looked up at me, for I was on slightly higher ground. When I asked them what they were doing here, the men looked at each other, and the first to recover from his surprise said, 'Nothing'. In reply to further questions, I was told that they were charcoal burners who had come from Bareilly and had lost their way. I then turned and looked towards the tree, and found that what I had taken to be gun barrels were stacked axes, the handles of which, polished by long and hard use, had reflected the firelight. Telling the men that my feet were wet and cold, I joined their circle, and after we had smoked my cigarettes and talked of many things, I directed them to the charcoal-burners' camp they were looking for, recovered my knife, and returned home.

In times of sustained excitement, imagination is apt to play queer tricks. Sitting on the ground near a sambhar killed by a tiger, I have heard the tiger coming and coming, and getting no nearer, and when the tension had become unbearable have turned round with finger on trigger to find a caterpillar biting minute bits out of a crisp leaf near my head. Again, when the light was fading and the time had come for the tiger to return to his kill, out of the corner of my eye I have seen a large animal appear; and as I was gripping my rifle and preparing for a shot, an ant had crawled out on a dry twig a few inches from my face. With my thoughts on Sultana, the glint of firelight on the polished axe-handles had converted them into gun barrels, and I never looked at them again until the men had convinced me they were charcoal burners.

With his efficient organization and better means of transport, Freddy was beginning to exert pressure on Sultana, and to ease the strain the dacoit leader took his gang, by this time considerably reduced by desertion and capture, to Pilibhit on the eastern border of the district. Here he remained for a few months, raiding as far afield as Gorakhpur and building up his store of gold.

On his return to the forests in our vicinity, he learned that a very rich dancing-girl from the State of Rampur had recently taken up residence with the headman of Lamachour, a village seven miles from our home. Anticipating a raid, the headman provided himself with a guard of thirty of his tenants. The guard was not armed, and when Sultana arrived, before his men were able to surround the house, the dancing-girl slipped through a back door and escaped into the night with all her jewellery. The headman and his tenants were rounded up in the courtyard, and when they denied all knowledge of the girl, orders were given to tie them up and beat them to refresh their memories. To this order one of the tenants raised an objection. He said Sultana could do what he liked to him and his fellow tenants, but that he had no right to disgrace the headman by having him tied up and beaten. He was ordered to keep his mouth shut, but as one of the dacoits advanced towards the headman with a length of rope, this intrepid man pulled a length of bamboo out of a lean-to and dashed at the dacoit. He was shot through the chest by one of the gang, but fearing the shot would arouse armed men in neighbouring villages Sultana beat a hasty retreat, taking with him a horse which the headman had recently purchased. I heard of the murder of the brave tenant next morning and sent one of my men to Lamachour to inquire what family the dead man had left, and I sent another man with an open letter to all the headmen of the surrounding villages to ask if they would join in raising a fund for the support of his family. The response to my appeal was as generous as I expected it to be, for the poor are always generous, but the fund was never raised, for the man who had given his life for his master, came from Nepal twenty years previously, and neither his friends nor the inquiries I made in Nepal revealed whether he had a wife or children.

It was after the incident just related that I accepted Freddy's invitation to take a hand in rounding up Sultana, and a month later I joined him at his headquarters at Haridwar. During his eighteen years as Collector of Mirzapur, Wyndham had employed ten Koles and ten Bhunyas from the tribes living in the Mirzapur forests to assist him in tiger shooting, and the four best of these men, who were old friends of mine, were now placed by Wyndham at Freddy's disposal and I found them waiting for me at Haridwar.

Freddy's plan was for my four friends and myself to track down Sultana, and when we had done this, to lead his force to a convenient place from which to launch his attack. Both these operations, for reasons already given, were to be carried out at night. But Sultana was restless. Perhaps it was just nervousness or he may have had forewarning of Freddy's plans; anyway he never stayed for more than a day in any one place, and he moved his force long distances at night.

The weather was intensely hot and eventually, tired of inaction, the four men and I held a council of war, the result of which was that after dinner that night, when Freddy was comfortably seated in a cool part of the veranda where there was no possibility of our being overheard, I put the following proposal before him. He was to let it be known that Wyndham had recalled his men for a tiger shoot, to which I had been invited, and was to have tickets to Haldwani purchased for us and see us off from the Haridwar station by the night train. At the first stop the train made, however, the four men, armed with guns provided by Freddy, and I with my own rifle were to leave the train. Thereafter we were to have a free hand to bring in Sultana, dead or alive, as opportunity offered.

Freddy sat for a long time with his eyes closed after hearing my proposal—he weighed 20 stone 4 pounds and was apt to doze after dinner—but he was not asleep, for he suddenly sat up and in a very decided voice said, 'No. I am responsible for your lives, and I won't sanction this mad 'scheme'. Arguing with him was of no avail, so the next morning the four men and I left for our respective homes. I was wrong to have made the proposal and Freddy was right in turning it down. The four men and I had no official standing, and had trouble resulted from our attempt to capture Sultana, our action could not have been justified. For the rest, neither Sultana's life nor ours was in any danger, for we had agreed that if Sultana could not be taken alive he would not be taken at all, and we were quite capable of looking after ourselves. Three months later, when the monsoon was in full blast, Freddy asked Herbert of the Forest Department, Fred Anderson, Superintendent of the Terai and Bhabar, and myself, to join him at Haridwar, On arrival we learnt that Freddy had located Sultana's permanent camp in the heart of the Najibabad jungles, and he wanted us to assist him in surrounding the camp, and to cut off Sultana's retreat if he slipped out of the ring.

Herbert, a famous polo player, was to be put in command of the fifty mounted men who were to prevent Sultana's escape, while Anderson and I were to accompany Freddy and help him to form the ring. By this time Freddy had no illusions about the efficiency of Sultana's intelligence service, and with the exception of Freddy's two assistants, and the three of us, no one knew of the contemplated raid. Each evening the police force, fully armed, were sent out on a long route march, while the four of us went out for an equally long walk, returning after dark to the Dam Bungalow in which we were staying. On the appointed night, instead of marching over the level crossing as they had been wont to do, the route marchers went through the Haridwar goods yard to a siding in which a rake of wagons, with engine and brake-van attached, was standing with doors open on the side away from the station buildings. The last of the doors was being shut as we arrived, and the moment we had climbed into the guard's van, the train, without any warning whistles, started. Everything that could be done to allay suspicion had been done, even to the cooking of the men's food in their lines and to the laying of our table for dinner. We had started an hour after dark. At 9 p.m. the train drew up between two stations in the heart of the jungle and the order was passed from wagon to wagon for the force to detrain, and as soon as this order had been carried out, the train steamed on.

Of Freddy's force of three hundred men, the fifty to be led by Herbert—who served in France in the First World War with the Indian cavalry—had been sent out the previous night with instructions to make a wide detour to where their mounts were waiting for them, while the main force of two hundred and fifty men with Freddy and Anderson in the lead, and myself bringing up the rear, set off for a destination which was said to be some twenty miles away. Heavy clouds had been banking up all day and when we left the train, it was raining in torrents.

Our direction was north for a mile, then east for two miles, again north for a mile, then west for two miles and finally again north. I knew the changes in direction were being made to avoid villages in which there were men in Sultana's pay, and the fact that not a village pye, the best watchdog in the world, barked at us testifies to the skill with which the manoeuvre was carried out. Hour after hour I plodded on, in drenching rain, in the wake of two hundred and fifty heavy men who had left pot holes in the soft ground into which I floundered up to my knees at every second step. For miles we went through elephant grass higher than my head, and balancing on the pitted and slippery ground became more difficult from the necessity of using one hand to shield my eyes from the stiff razor-edged grass. I had often marvelled at

Freddy's 20 stone 4 pounds of energy, but never as I did that night. True, he was walking on comparatively firm ground while I was walking in a bog; yet even so, he was carrying nine stone more than I, and the line moved on with never a halt.

We had started at 9 p.m. At 2 a.m. I sent a verbal message up the line to ask Freddy if we were going in the right direction. I sent this message because for an hour we had left our original direction northwards, and had been going east. After a long interval, word came back that the Captain Sahib said it was all right. After another two hours, through thick tree and scrub jungle or across patches of high grass, I sent a second message to Freddy asking him to halt the line as I was coming up to speak to him. Silence had been enjoined before starting, and as I made my way to the front I passed a very quiet and weary line of men, some of them sitting on the wet ground and others leaning against trees.

I found Freddy and Anderson with their four guides at the head of the column. When Freddy asked if anything was wrong—this I knew referred to stragglers—I said all was well with the men but otherwise everything was wrong, for we were walking in circles. Having lived so much of my life in jungles in which it is very easy to get lost I have acquired a sense of direction which functions as well by night as it does by day. Our change of direction when we first started had been as evident to me as it had been two hours back when we changed direction from north to east. In addition, an hour previously I had noted that we passed under a simul tree with a vulture's nest in it, and when I sent my message to Freddy to halt the line, I was again under the same tree.

Of the four guides, two were Bhantus of Sultana's gang who had been captured a few days previously in the Haridwar bazaar, and on whose information the present raid had been organized. These two men had lived off and on for two years in Sultana's camp and had been promised their freedom for this night's work. The other two were cattle men who had grazed their cattle in these jungles all their lives, and who daily supplied Sultana with milk. All four men stoutly denied having lost their way, but on being pressed, they hesitated, and finally admitted that they would feel happier about the direction in which they were leading the force if they could see the hills. To see the hills, possibly thirty miles away, on a dark night with thick fog descending down to tree-top level, was impossible, so here was a check which threatened to ruin all Freddy's well-laid plans and, what was even worse, to give Sultana the laugh on us. Our intention had been a surprise attack on the camp, and in order to accomplish this, it was necessary to get within striking distance while it was still dark. The guides had informed us that it was not possible to approach the camp in daylight from the side we had chosen without being seen by two guards who were constantly on watch from a machan in a high tree which overlooked a wide stretch of grass to the south of the camp. With our guides now freely admitting they had lost their way, only another hour of darkness left and, worst of all, without knowing how far we were from the camp or in which direction it lay, our chance of a surprise attack was receding with every minute that passed. Then a way out of the dilemma occurred to me. I asked the four men if there was any feature, such as a stream or a well-defined cattle-track, in the direction in which we had originally started, by which they could regain direction, and when they replied that there was an old and well-defined cart-track a mile to the south of the camp, I obtained Freddy's permission to take the lead. I set off at a fast pace in a direction which all who were following me were, I am sure, convinced would lead back to the railway line we had left seven hours earlier.

The rain had stopped, a fresh breeze had cleared the sky of clouds, and it was just getting light in the east when I stumbled into a deep cart-rut. Here was the disused track the guides had mentioned, and their joy on seeing it confirmed the opinion I had formed earlier, that losing themselves in the jungle had not been intentional. Taking over the lead again, the men led us along the track for a mile to where a well-used game-track crossed it. Half a mile up the game- track we came to a deep and sluggish stream some thirty feet wide which I was glad to see the track did not cross, for I am terrified of these Terai streams, on the banks and in the depths of which I have seen huge pythons lurking. The track skirted the right bank of the stream, through shoulder-high grass, and after going along it for a few hundred yards, the men slowed down. From the way they kept looking to the left I concluded we were getting within sight of the machan, for it was now full daylight with the sun touching the tops of the trees. Presently the leading man crouched down, and when his companions had done the same, he beckoned us to approach.

After signalling to the line to halt and sit down, Freddy, Anderson and I crept up to the leading guide. Lying beside him and looking through the grass in the direction in which he was pointing we saw a machan built in the upper branches of a big tree, between thirty and forty feet above ground. On the machan, with the level sun shining on them, were two men, one sitting with his right shoulder towards us smoking a hookah, and the other lying on his back with his knees drawn up. The tree in which the machan was built was growing on the border of the tree and grass jungle and overlooked a wide expanse of open ground. Sultana's camp, the guides said, was three hundred yards inside the tree jungle.

A few feet from where we were lying was a strip of short grass twenty yards wide, running from the stream on our right far out on to the open ground. To retreat a little, cross the stream, and recross it opposite Sultana's camp was the obvious thing to do, but the guides said this would not be possible; not only was the stream too deep to wade, but there was quicksand along the far bank. There remained the doubtful possibility of getting the whole force across the strip of short grass without being seen by the two guards, either of whom might at any moment look in our direction.

Freddy had a service revolver, Anderson was unarmed and I was the only one in the whole force who was carrying a rifle—the police were armed with 12-bore muskets using buckshot, with an effective range of sixty to eighty yards. I was therefore the only one of the party who could deal with the two guards from our present position. The rifle shots would, of course, be heard in the camp, but the two Bhantus with us were of the opinion that when the guards did not return to the camp to report, men would be sent out to make inquiries. They thought that while this was being done, it would be possible for us to encircle the camp.

The two men on the machan were outlaws, and quite possibly murderers to boot, and with the rifle in my hands I could have shot the hookah out of the smoker's hands and the heel off the other man's shoe without injury to either.

But to shoot the men in cold, or in any other temperature of blood, was beyond my powers. So I made the following alternative suggestion: that Freddy give me permission to stalk the men—which would be quite easy, for the tall grass and tree jungle extended right up to the tree in which the machan was built and was soaking wet after the all-night rain—and occupy the machan with them while Freddy and his men carried on with their job. At first Freddy demurred, for there were two guns on the machan within easy reach of the men's hands, but eventually he consented and without further ado I slipped across the open ground and set off, for the Bhantus said the time was approaching for the guards to be changed.

I had covered about a third of the way to the tree when I heard a noise behind and saw Anderson hurrying after me. What Anderson had said to Freddy, or Freddy had said to Anderson I do not know—both were my very good friends. Anyway, Anderson was determined to accompany me. He admitted he could not get through the jungle silently; that there was a good chance of the men on the machan hearing and seeing us; that we might run into the relief guard or find additional guards at the foot of the tree; that being unarmed he would not be able to defend himself, nevertheless and not withstanding, he was not going to let me go alone. When a man from across the Clyde digs his toes in, he is more stubborn than a mule.

In desperation I started to retrace my steps to solicit Freddy's help. But Freddy in the meantime had had time to regret his sanction (I learnt later the Bhantus had informed him the men on the machan were very good shots), and when he saw us returning, he gave the signal for the line to advance.

Fifty or more men had crossed the open strip of ground and we, who were in advance, were within two hundred yards of the camp when a zealous young constable, catching sight of the machan, fired off his musket. The two men on the machan were down the ladder in a flash. They mounted the horses that were tethered at the foot of the tree and raced for the camp. There was now no longer any necessity for silence and in a voice that did not need the aid of a megaphone, Freddy gave the order to charge. In a solid line we swept down on the camp, to find it deserted.

The camp was on a little knoll and consisted of three tents and a grass hut used as a kitchen. One of the tents was a store and was stacked with sacks of atta, rice, dal, sugar, tins of ghee, two pyramids of boxes containing some thousands of rounds of 12-bore ammunition, and eleven guns in gun cases. The other two tents were sleeping places and were strewn with blankets and a medley of articles of clothing. Hanging from branches near the kitchen were three flayed goats.

In the confusion following the arrival in camp of the two guards it was possible that some of the partly clothed gang had taken shelter in the high grass surrounding the camp, so orders were given to our men to make a long line, our intention being to beat a wide strip of jungle in the direction in which Herbert and his mounted men were on guard. While the line was being formed, I made a cast round the knoll. Having found the tracks of ten or a dozen barefooted men in a nullah close to the camp, I suggested to Freddy that we should follow them and see where they led to. The nullah was fifteen feet wide and five feet deep, and Freddy, Anderson and I had proceeded along it for about two hundred yards when we came on an outcrop of gravel, where I lost the tracks. Beyond the gravel, the nullah opened out and on the left bank, near where we were standing, was a giant banyan tree with multiple stems. With its forest of stems, and branches sweeping down to the ground, this tree appeared to me to be an ideal place for anyone to hide in, so going to the bank, which at this point was as high as my chin, I attempted to climb up. There was no handhold on the bank and each time I kicked a hole in the soft earth the foothold gave way, and I was just contemplating going forward and getting on to the bank where the nullah rattened out, when a fusillade of shots followed by shouting, broke out in the direction of the camp. We dashed back the way we had come and near the camp, found a Havildar shot through the chest, and near him a dacoit, with a wisp of cloth round his loins, shot through both legs. The Havildar was sitting on the ground with his back to a tree; his shirt was open, and on the nipple of his left breast there was a spot of blood. Freddy produced a flask and put it to the Havildar's lips, but the man shook his head and put the flask aside, saying, 'It is wine. I cannot drink it'. When pressed, he added, 'All my life I have been an abstainer, and I cannot go to my Creator with wine on my lips. I am thirsty and crave a little water'. His brother was standing near by. Someone gave him a hat and he dashed off to the stream that had hampered our movements, and returned in a few minutes with some dirty water which the wounded man drank eagerly. The wound had been made by a pellet of shot and when I could not feel it under the skin, I said, 'Keep a strong heart, Havildar Sahib, and the doctor at Najibabad will make you well'. Smiling up at me he replied, 'I will keep a strong heart, Sahib; but no doctor can make me well'.

The dacoit had no inhibitions about 'wine,' and in a few gulps he emptied the contents of the flask of which he was in great need, for he had been shot with a 12-bore musket at very short range.

Two stretchers were improvised from material taken

from Sultana's camp, and willing hands—for no distinction was made between the high-caste member of the police force and the low-caste dacoit—took them up. With spare runners running alongside, the stretchers set off through the jungle for the Najibabad hospital twelve miles away. The dacoit died of loss of blood and of shock on the way, and the Havildar died a few minutes after being admitted to the hospital.

The beat was abandoned. Herbert did not come into the picture, for Sultana had been warned of the concentration of horse and none of the dacoits tried to cross the line he was guarding. So the sum total of our carefully planned raid, which had miscarried through no one's fault, was Sultana's entire camp less a few guns, and two dead men—one a poor man, who, chafing at confinement, had sough liberty and adopted the only means of livelihood open to him and who would be mourned by a widow in the Najibabad fort, and the other, a man respected by his superiors and loved by his men, whose widow would be cared for, and who had bravely died for a principle, for the 'wine' with which he refused to defile his lips would have sustained him until he had been laid on the operating table.

Three days after the raid, Freddy received a letter from the dacoit leader in which Sultana regretted that a shortage of arms and ammunition in the police force had necessitated a raid on his camp, and stating that if in future, Freddy would let him know his requirements he, Sultana, would be very glad to supply him.

The supply of arms and ammunition to Sultana was a very sore point with Freddy. Stringent orders on the subject had been issued, but it was not surprising that every licensed dealer and every licensed gun-holder in the area in which

Sultana was operating was willing to risk the Government's displeasure when the alternative was the certainty of having his house raided, and the possibility of having his throat cut, if he refused Sultana's demands. So the offer of arms and ammunition was no idle one and it was the most unkind cut the dacoit leader could have delivered to the head of the Special Dacoity Police Force.

With his hide-out gone, harried from end to end of the Terai and Bhabar, and with his gang reduced to forty—all well armed, for the dacoits had soon replaced the arms and ammunition taken from them—Freddy thought the time had now come for Sultana to surrender. So, after obtaining Government sanction—which was given on the understanding that he personally accepted full responsibility—he invited Sultana to a meeting, whenever and wherever convenient. Sultana accepted the invitation, named the time, date and place, and stipulated that both should attend the meeting alone and unarmed. On the appointed day, as Freddy stepped out on one side of a wide open glade, in the centre of which a solitary tree was growing, Sultana stepped out on the other side. Their meeting was friendly, as all who have lived in the East would have expected it to be, and when they had seated themselves in the shade of the tree—one a mountain of energy and good humour with the authority of the Government behind him, and the other a dapper little man with a price on his head—Sultana produced a watermelon which he smilingly said Freddy could partake of without reservation. The meeting ended in a deadlock, however, for Sultana refused to accept Freddy's terms of unconditional surrender. It was at this meeting that Sultana begged Freddy not to take undue risks. On the day of the raid, he said, he, with ten of his men, all fully armed, had taken cover under a banyan tree and had watched Freddy and two other sahibs coming down the nullah towards the tree. 'Had the sahib who was trying to climb the bank succeeded in doing so', Sultana added, 'it would have been necessary to shoot the three of you.'

The final round of the heavy-light-weight contest was now to be staged, and Freddy invited Wyndham and I, myself, to Haridwar to witness and take part in it. Sultana and the remnants of his gang, now weary of movement, had taken up residence at a cattle station in the heart of the Najibabad jungles, and Freddy's plan was to convey his entire force down the Ganges in boats, land at a convenient spot, and surround the cattle station. This raid, like the one already described, was to take place at night. But on this occasion, the raid had been timed for the full moon.

On the day chosen, the entire force of three hundred men, with the addition of Freddy's cousin, Wyndham, and myself, embarked as night was falling in ten country boats which had been assembled at a secluded spot on the right bank of the Ganges, a few miles below Haridwar. I was in the leading boat, and all went well until we crossed to the left bank and entered a side channel. The passage down this channel was one of the most terrifying experiences, off dry land, that I have ever had. For a few hundred yards the boat glided over a wide expanse of moonlit water without a ripple on its surface to distort the reflection of the trees on the margin. Gradually the channel narrowed and the speed of the boat increased, and at the same time we heard the distant sound of rushing water. I have often fished in these side channels of the Ganges, for they are preferred to the main stream by fish, and I marvelled at the courage of the boatmen who were willing to risk their lives and their craft in the rapids we were fast approaching. The boat, like the other nine, was an open cargo freighter eminently suitable for work on the open Ganges, but here in this narrow swift-flowing channel, she was just an unmanageable hulk, which threatened to become a wreck every time her bottom planks came in violent contact with submerged boulders. The urgent call of the captain to his crew to fend the boat off the rocky banks and keep her in the middle of the stream, or she would founder, did nothing to allay my fears, for at the time the warning was given, the boat was drifting sideways and threatening to break up or capsize every time she struck the bottom. But nightmares cannot last for ever. Though the one that night was long-drawn-out, for we had twenty miles to go, mostly through broken water, it ended when one of the boatmen sprang ashore on the left bank with one end of a long rope and made it fast to a tree. Boat after boat passed us and tied up lower down, until all ten had been accounted for.

The force was disembarked on a sandy beach and when cuts and abrasions resulting from contact with the rough timbers of the boats had been attended to, and the boatmen had been instructed to take their craft five miles farther down stream and await orders, we set off in single file to battle our way through half a mile of the heaviest elephant grass I have ever tried to penetrate on foot. The grass was ten to twelve feet high and was weighted down with river fog and dew, and before we had gone a hundred yards we were wet to the skin. When we eventually arrived on the far side, we were faced with a wide expanse of water which we took to be an old bed of the Ganges, and scouting parties were sent right and left to find the shortest way round the obstruction. The party that had gone to the right returned first and reported that a quarter of a mile from where we were standing the 'lake' narrowed, and that from this point to the junction of the channel down which we had come, there was a swift- flowing river. Soon after the other party returned and reported that there was an unfordable river flowing into the upper end of the lake. It was now quite evident that our boatmen, intentionally or accidentally, had marooned us on an island.

With our boats gone and daylight not far off, it was necessary to do something, so we moved down to the lower end of the wide expanse of water to see if we could effect a crossing between it and the junction of the two channels. Where the water narrowed and the toe or draw of the stream started, there appeared to be a possible crossing; above this point the water was twenty feet deep, and below it was a raging torrent. While the rest of us were looking at the fast-flowing water and speculating as to whether anyone would be able to cross it, Wyndham was divesting himself of his clothes. When I remarked that this was an unnecessary proceeding in view of the fact that he was already wet to the skin, he replied that he was not thinking of his clothes, but of his life. When he had taken off every stitch of clothing, he tied it into a bundle, using his shirt for the purpose, and placed the bundle firmly on his head, caught the arm of a strapping young constable standing near by and said, 'Come with me'. The young man was so taken aback at being selected to have the honour of drowning with the Commissioner Sahib that he said nothing, and together, with linked arms, the two stepped into the water.

I do not think any of us breathed while we watched that crossing. With the water at times round their waists, and at times up to their armpits, it seemed impossible for them to avoid being carried off their feet and swept into the raging torrent below where no man, no matter how good a swimmer he was, could have lived. Steadily the two brave men, one, the oldest in the party, and the other, possibly the youngest, fought their way on, and when at last they struggled out on the far bank, a sigh of relief went up from the spectators, which would have been a cheer audible in Haridwar, twenty miles away, had silence not been imposed on us.

Where two men could go three hundred could follow, so a chain was made; and though individual links were at times swept off their feet, the chain held, and the whole force landed safely on the far side. Here we were met by one of Freddy's most trusted informers who, pointing to the rising sun, said we had come too late; that it would not be possible for such a large force to cross the open ground between us and the forest without being seen by the herdsmen in the area, and that therefore the only thing for us to do was to go back to the island. So back to the island we went, the crossing from this side not being as bad as it had been from the other.

Back in the elephant grass our first concern was to dry our clothes. This was soon accomplished, for the sun was by now hot, and when we were once again dry and warm, Freddy, from his capacious haversack, produced a chicken and a loaf of bread which were no less welcome for having been immersed in the cold waters of the Ganges. I have the ability to sleep anywhere and at any time, and, having found a sandy hollow, most of the day had passed when I was awakened by violent sneezing. On joining my companions I found that all three of them were suffering from varying degrees of hay fever. The grass we were in was of the plumed variety and when we had passed through it in the early morning, the plumes had been wet. But now, in the hot sun, the plumes had fluffed out and while moving about and trying to find cool places to rest in, my companions had shaken the pollen down, with the result that they had given themselves hay fever.

Indians do not get hay fever and I myself have never had it. This was the first time I had ever seen anyone suffering from it, and what I saw alarmed me. Freddy's cousin—a planter on holiday from Bengal—was the worst of the three; his eyes were streaming and swollen to the extent that he could not see, and his nose was running. Freddy could see a little but he could not stop sneezing, and when Freddy sneezed, the earth shook. Wyndham, tough old campaigner that he was, while protesting that he was quite all right, was unable to keep his handkerchief away from his nose and eyes. It was bad enough being thrown about in an open boat, marooned on a desert island, and fording raging torrents; but here was the climax. To lead three men who threatened to go blind back to Haridwar at the head of the three hundred policemen was a prospect that made me feel colder than I had felt when crossing the ice-cold waters of the Ganges. As evening closed in, the condition of the sufferers improved, much to my relief, and by the time we had crossed the ford for the third time, Freddy and Wyndham were all right and the cousin had regained his sight to the extent that it was no longer necessary to tell him when to raise his foot to avoid a stone. Freddy's informer and a guide were waiting for us and led us over the open ground to the mouth of a dry watercourse about a hundred yards wide. The moon had just risen and visibility was nearly as good as in sunlight when, rounding a bend, we came face to face with an elephant. We had heard there was a rogue elephant in this area, and here he was, tusks flashing in the moonlight, ears spread out, and emitting loud squeals. The guide did nothing to improve the situation by stating that the elephant was very bad tempered, that he had killed many people, and that he was sure to kill a number of us. At first it appeared that the rogue was going to make good the guide's predictions, for with trunk raised high he advanced a few yards. Then he swung round and dashed up the bank, trumpeting defiance as he gained the shelter of the jungle.

Another mile up the watercourse and we came on what the guide said was a fire-track. Here the going was very pleasant, for with short green grass underfoot, and the moonlight glinting on every leaf and blade, it was possible to forget our errand and revel in the beauty of the jungle. As we approached a stretch of burnt grass where an old peacock, perched high on a leafless tree, was sending his warning cry into the night, two leopards stepped out on the track, saw us, and gracefully bounded away and faded out of sight in the shadows. I had been out of my element during the long passage down the side channel, but now, what with the elephant—who was, I knew, only curious and intended us no harm—and then the peacock warning the jungle folk of the presence of danger, and finally the leopards merging into the shadows, I was back on familiar ground—ground that I loved and understood.

Leaving the track, which ran from east to west, the guide led us north for a mile or more through scrub and tree jungle to the bank of a tiny stream overhung by a giant banyan tree. Here we were told to sit down and wait, while the guide went forward to confer with his brother at the cattle station. A long and weary wait it was, which was in no way relieved by pangs of hunger, for we had eaten nothing since our meal off the chicken and loaf of bread, and it was now past midnight; and to make matters worse, I, the only one who smoked, had exhausted my supply of cigarettes. The guide returned towards the early hours of the morning and reported that Sultana and the remnants of his gang, now reduced to nine, had left the cattle station the previous evening to raid a village in the direction of Haridwar and that they were expected back that night, or the following day. Before leaving to try to get us a little food, of which we were in urgent need, the guide and the informer warned us that we were in Sultana's territory and that it would be unwise for any of us to leave the shelter of the banyan tree.

Another weary day passed, the last Wyndham could spend with us, for in addition to being Commissioner of Kumaon he was Political Agent of Tehri State and was due to meet the ruler at Narindra Nagar in two days time.

After nightfall, a cart loaded with grass arrived, and when the grass had been removed, a few sacks of parched gram and forty pounds of gur were revealed. This scanty but welcome ration was distributed among the men. The guide had not forgotten the sahibs, and before driving away, he handed Freddy a few chapattis tied up in a piece of cloth that had seen hard times and better days. As we lay on our backs with all topics of conversation exhausted, thinking of hot meals and soft beds in far-off Haridwar, I heard the welcome sounds of a leopard killing a chital a few hundred yards from our tree. Here was an opportunity of getting a square meal, for my portion of chapatti, far from allaying my hunger, had only added to it; so I jumped up and asked Freddy for his kukri. When he asked what on earth I wanted it for, I told him it was to cut off the hind legs of the chital the leopard had just killed. 'What leopard and what chital', he asked, 'are you talking about?' Yes, he could hear the chital calling, but how was he to know that they were not alarmed by some of Sultana's men who were scouting round to spy on us? And anyway, if I was right in thinking a leopard had made a kill, which he doubted, how was I going to take the chital away from it when I could not use a musket (I had not brought my rifle with me on this occasion for I did not know to what use I might be asked to put it) so close to the cattle station? No, he concluded, the whole idea was absurd. So very regretfully I again lay down with my hunger. How could I convince anyone who did not know the jungle folk and their language that I knew the deer had not been alarmed by human beings; that they were watching one of their number being killed by a leopard; and that there was no danger in taking the kill, or as much of it as I wanted, away from the leopard?

The night passed without further incident and at crack of dawn, Wyndham and I set out on our long walk to Haridwar. We crossed the Ganges by the Bhimgoda Dam and after a quick meal at the Dam Bungalow, had an evening's fishing on the wide expanse of water above the dam that will long be remembered.

Next morning, just as Wyndham was leaving to keep his appointment at Narindra Nagar, and I was collecting some eatables to take back to my hungry companions, word was brought to us by a runner that Freddy had captured Sultana. Sultana had returned to the cattle station the previous evening. After his men had surrounded the station, Freddy crept up to the large hut used by the cattle men, and, seeing a sheeted figure asleep on the only charpoy the hut contained, sat down on it. Pinned down by 20 stone 4 pounds, Sultana was not unable to offer any resistance, nor was he able to carry out his resolve of not being taken alive. Of the six dacoits in the hut at the time of the raid, four, including Sultana, were captured and the other two, Babu and Pailwan, Sultana's lieutenants, broke through the police cordon and escaped, after being fired at.

I do not know how many murders Sultana was responsible for, but when brought to trial, the main charge against him was the murder, by one of his gang, of the tenant of the headman of Lamachour. While in the condemned cell, Sultana sent for Freddy and bequeathed to him his wife and son in the Najibabad Fort, and his dog, of whom he was very fond. Freddy adopted the dog, and those who know Freddy will not need to be told that he faithfully carried out his promise to care for Sultana's family.

Some months later, Freddy, now promoted and the youngest man in the Indian Police service ever to be honoured by His Majesty the King with a C.I.E., was attending the annual Police Week at Moradabad. One of the functions at this week was a dinner to which all the police officers in the province were invited. During the dinner, one of the waiters whispered to Freddy that his orderly wanted to speak to him. This orderly had been with Freddy during the years Freddy had been in pursuit of Sultana. Now, having an evening off, he had strolled down to the Moradabad railway station. While he was there, a train came in, and as he idly watched the passengers alighting, two men came out of a compartment near him. One of these men spoke to the other, who hastily put a handkerchief up to his face, but not before the orderly had seen that he had a piece of cotton wool sticking to his nose. The orderly kept his eye on the men, who had a considerable amount of luggage, and when they had made themselves comfortable in a corner of the waiting room, he commandeered an ekka and hastened to inform Freddy. When Sultana's two lieutenants,

Babu and Pailwan, broke through the cordon surrounding the cattle station, they had been fired at, and shortly thereafter a man had visited a small dispensary near Najibabad to have an injury to his nose, which he said had been caused by a dog bite, attended to. When reporting the case to the police, the compounder who dressed the wound said he suspected it had been caused by a pellet of buckshot. So the entire police force of the province were on the lookout for a man with an injured nose, all the more so because Babu and Pailwan were credited with having committed most of the murders for which Sultana's gang were responsible.

When he heard the orderly's story, Freddy jumped into his car and dashed to the station—dashed is the right word, for when Freddy is in a hurry, the road is before him and traffic and corners do not exist. At the station he placed guards at all the exits to the waiting room and then went up to the two men and asked them who they were. Merchants, they answered, on their way from Bareilly to Punjab. Why then, asked Freddy, had they taken a train that terminated at Moradabad? He was told that there had been two trains at the Bareilly platform and they had been directed to the wrong one. When Freddy learnt the men had not had any food, and that they would have to wait until next morning for a connecting train, he invited them to accompany him and be his guests. For a moment the men hesitated, and then said,

'As you wish, Sahib.'

With the two men in the back of the car Freddy drove slowly, closely questioning them, and to all his questions he received prompt answers. The men then asked Freddy if it was customary for sahibs to visit railway stations at night and carry off passengers, leaving their luggage to be plundered by any who cared to do so. Freddy knew that his action, without a duly executed warrant, could be described as high-handed and might land him in serious trouble if the members of Sultana's gang serving sentences in the Moradabad jail failed to identify their late companions. While these unpleasant thoughts were chasing each other through his mind, the car arrived at the bungalow in which he was putting up for the Police Week. All dogs love Freddy, and Sultana's dog was no exception. In the months that had passed, this pye with a dash of terrier blood had given Freddy all his affection, and now, when the car stopped and the three men got out, the dog came dashing out of the bungalow, stopped in surprise, and then hurled himself at the two travellers with every manifestation of delight that a dog can exhibit. For a tense minute, Freddy and the two men looked at each other in silence and then Pailwan, who knew the fate that awaited him, stooped down and patting the dog's head said, 'In face of this honest witness what use is it, Young Sahib, for us to deny we are the men you think we are?'.

Society demands protection against criminals, and Sultana was a criminal. He was tried under the law of the land, found guilty and executed. Nevertheless, I cannot withhold a great measure of admiration for the little man who set at nought the might of the Government for three long years, and who, by his brave demeanour, won the respect of those who guarded him in the condemned cell.

I could have wished that justice had not demanded that Sultana be exhibited in manacles and leg-irons, and exposed to ridicule from those who trembled at the mere mention of his name while he was at liberty. I could also have wished that he had been given a more lenient sentence, for no other reasons than that he had been branded a criminal at birth, and had not had a fair chance; that when power was in his hands, he had not oppressed the poor; that when I tracked him to the banyan tree, he spared my life and the lives of my friends. And finally, that he went to his meeting with Freddy, not armed with a knife or a revolver, but with a watermelon in his hands.

8

Loyalty

The mail train was running at its maximum speed of thirty miles per hour through country that was familiar. For mile upon mile the newly risen sun had been shining on fields where people were reaping the golden wheat, for it was the month of April and the train was passing through the Gangetic valley, the most fertile land in India.

During the previous year India had witnessed one of her worst famines. I had seen whole villages existing on the bark of trees, on minute grass seeds swept up with infinite labour from scorching plains, and on the wild plums that grow on waste lands too poor for the raising of crops. Mercifully the weather had changed, good winter rains had brought back fertility to the land, and the people who had starved for a year, were now eagerly reaping a good harvest. Early though the hour was, the scene was one of intense activity in which every individual of the community had his, or her, allotted part. The reaping was being done by women, most of them landless labourers who move from area to area, as the crop ripens, and who, for their labour—which starts at dawn and ends when there is no longer light to work by—receive one-twelfth to one-sixteenth of the crop they cut in the course of the day.

There were no hedges to obstruct the view, and from the carriage window no mechanical device of any kind was to be seen. The ploughing had been done by oxen, two to a plough; the reaping was being done by sickles with a curved blade eighteen inches long; the sheaves, tied with twisted stalks of wheat straw, were being carted to the threshing floor on ox-carts with wooden wheels; and on the threshing floor, plastered over with cow dung, oxen were treading out the corn; they were tied to a long rope, one end of which was made fast to a pole firmly fixed in the ground. As a field was cleared of the sheaves, children drove cattle on to it to graze on the stubble and amongst the cattle, old and infirm women were sweeping the ground to recover any seed that had fallen from the ears when the wheat was being cut. Half of what these toilers collected would be taken by the owner of the field and the other half—which might amount to as much as a pound or two, if the ground was not too sun-cracked— they would be permitted to retain.

My journey was to last for thirty-six hours. I had the carriage to myself, and the train would stop for breakfast, lunch and dinner. Every mile of the country through which the train was running was interesting; and yet I was not happy, for in the steel trunk under my seat was a string bag containing two hundred rupees which did not belong to me.

Eighteen months previously I had taken employment as a Fuel Inspector with the railway on which I was now travelling. I had gone straight from school to this job, and for those eighteen months I had lived in the forest cutting five hundred thousand cubic feet of timber, to be used as fuel in locomotives. After the trees had been felled and billeted, each billet not more and not less than thirty-six inches long, the fuel was carted ten miles to the nearest point of the railway, where it was stacked and measured and then loaded into fuel trains and taken to the stations where it was needed. Those eighteen months alone in the forest had been strenuous, but I had kept fit and enjoyed the work. There was plenty of game in the forest in the way of chital, four-horned antelope, pig and peafowl, and in the river that formed one boundary of the forest there were several varieties of fish and many alligators and python. My work did not permit of my indulging in sport during daylight hours so I had to do all my shooting for the pot, and fishing, at night. Shooting by moonlight is very different from shooting in daylight, for though it is easier to stalk a deer or a rooting pig at night, it is difficult to shoot accurately unless the moon can be got to shine on the foresight. The peafowl had to be shot while they were roosting, and I am not ashamed to say that I occasionally indulged in this form of murder, for the only meat I ate during that year and a half was what I shot on moonlight nights; during the dark period of the moon I had perforce to be a vegetarian.

The felling of the forest disarranged the normal life of the jungle folk and left me with the care of many waifs and orphans, all of whom had to share my small tent with me. It was when I was a bit crowded with two broods of partridges—one black and the other grey, four peafowl chicks, two leverets, and two baby four-horned antelope that could only just stand upright on their spindle legs, that Rex the python took up his quarters in the tent. I returned an hour after nightfall that day, and while I was feeding the four-footed inmates with milk I saw the lantern light glinting on something in a corner of the tent and on investigation found Rex coiled up on the straw used as a bed by the baby antelope. A hurried count revealed that none of the young inmates of the tent were missing, so I left Rex in the corner he had selected. For two months thereafter Rex left the tent each day to bask in the sun, returning to his corner at sundown, and during the whole of that period he never harmed any of the young life he shared the tent with.

Of all the waifs and orphans who were brought up in the tent, and who were returned to the forest as soon as they were able to fend for themselves, Tiddley-de-winks, a four-horned antelope, was the only one who refused to leave me. She followed me when I moved camp to be nearer to the railway line to supervise the loading of the fuel, and in doing so nearly lost her life. Having been brought up by hand she had no fear of human beings and the day after our move she approached a man who, thinking she was a wild animal, tried to kill her. When I returned to the tent that evening I found her lying near my camp bed and on picking her up saw that both her forelegs had been broken, and that the broken ends of the bones had worked through the skin. While I was getting a little milk down her throat, and trying to summon sufficient courage to do what I knew should be done, my servant came into the tent with a man who admitted to having tried to kill the poor beast. It appeared that this man had been working in his field when Tiddley-de-winks went up to him, and thinking she had strayed in from the nearby forest, he struck her with a stick and then chased her, and it was only when she entered my tent that he realized she was a tame animal. My servant had advised him to leave before I returned, but this the man had refused to do. When he had told his story he said he would return early next morning with a bone-setter from his village. There was nothing I could do for the injured animal, beyond making a soft bed for her and giving her milk at short intervals, and at day break next morning the man returned with the bone-setter.

It is unwise in India to judge from appearances. The bone-setter was a feeble old man, exhibiting in his person and tattered dress every sign of poverty, but he was none the less a specialist, and a man of few words. He asked me to lift up the injured animal, stood looking at her for a few minutes, and then turned and left the tent, saying over his shoulder that he would be back in two hours. I had worked week in week out for months on end so I considered I was justified in taking a morning off, and before the old man returned I had cut a number of stakes in the nearby jungle and constructed a small pen in a corner of the tent. The man brought back with him a number of dry jute stalks from which the bark had been removed, a quantity of green paste, several young castor-oil plant leaves as big as plates and a roll of thin jute twine. When I had seated myself on the edge of the camp bed with Tiddley-de-winks across my knees, her weight partly supported by her hind legs and partly by my knees, the old man sat down on the ground in front of her with his materials within reach.

The bones of both forelegs had been splintered midway between the knees and the tiny hooves, and the dangling portion of the legs had twisted round and round. Very gently the old man untwisted the legs, covered them from knee to hoof with a thick layer of green paste, laid strips of the castor-oil leaves over the paste to keep it in position, and over the leaves laid the jute stalks, binding them to the legs with jute twine. Next morning he returned with splints made of jute stalks strung together, and when they had been fitted to her legs Tiddley-de-winks was able to bend her knees and place her hooves, which extended an inch beyond the splints, on the ground.

The bone-setter's fee was one rupee, plus two annas for the ingredients he had put in the paste and the twine he had purchased in the bazaar and not until the splints had been removed and the little antelope was able to skip about again would he accept either his fee or the little present I gratefully offered him.

My work, every day of which I had enjoyed, was over now and I was on my way to headquarters to render an account of the money I had spent and, I feared, to look for another job; for the locomotives had been converted to coal-burning and no more wood fuel would be needed. My books were all in perfect order and I had the feeling that I had rendered good service, for I had done in eighteen months what had been estimated to take two years. Yet I was uneasy, and the reason for my being so was the bag of money in my steel trunk.

I reached my destination, Samastipur, at 9 a.m. and after depositing my luggage in the waiting-room, set out for the office of the head of the department I had been working for, with my account books and the bag containing the two hundred rupees. At the office I was told by a very imposing doorkeeper that the master was engaged, and that I would have to wait. It was hot in the open veranda, and as the minutes dragged by my nervousness increased, for an old railway hand who had helped me to make up my book shad warned me that to submit balanced accounts and then admit, as I had every intention of doing, that I had two hundred rupees in excess would land me in very great trouble. Eventually the door opened and a very harassed-looking man emerged; and before the doorkeeper could close it, a voice from inside the room bellowed at me to come in.

Ryles, the head of the Locomotive Department of the Bengal and North Western Railway, was a man weighing sixteen stone, with a voice that struck terror into all who served under him, and with a heart of gold. Bidding me sit down he drew my books towards him, summoned a clerk and very carefully checked my figures with those received from the stations to which the fuel had been sent. Then he told me he regretted my services would no longer be needed, said that discharge orders would be sent to me later in the day, and indicated that the interview was over. Having picked my hat off the floor I started to leave, but was called back and told I had forgotten to remove what appeared to be a bag of money that I had placed on the table. It was foolish of me to have thought I could just leave the two hundred rupees and walk away, but that was what I was trying to do when Ryles called me; so I went back to the table and told him that the money belonged to the Railway, and as I did not know how to account for it in my books, I had brought it to him. 'Your books are balanced', Ryles said, 'and if you have not faked your accounts I should like an explanation.' Tewari, the head clerk, had come into the room with a tray of papers and he stood behind Ryles's chair, with encouragement in his kindly old eyes, as I gave Ryles the following explanation.

When my work was nearing completion, fifteen cart-men, who had been engaged to cart fuel from the forest to the railway line, came to me one night and stated they had received an urgent summons to return to their village, to harvest the crops. The fuel they had carted was scattered over a wide area, and as it would take several days to stack and measure it they wanted me to make a rough calculation of the amount due to them, as it was essential for them to start on their journey that night. It was a dark night and quite impossible for me to calculate the cubic contents of the fuel, so I told them I would accept their figures. Two hours later they returned, and within a few minutes of paying them, I heard their carts creaking away into the night. They left no address with me, and several weeks later, when the fuel was stacked and measured, I found they had underestimated the amount due to them by two hundred rupees.

When I had told my story Ryles informed me that the Agent, Izat, was expected in Samastipur next day, and that he would leave him to deal with me. Izat, Agent of three of the most flourishing railways in India, arrived next morning and at midday I received a summons to attend Ryles's office. Izat, a small dapper man with piercing eyes, was alone in the office when I entered it, and after complimenting me on having finished my job six months ahead of time he said Ryles had shown him my books and given him a report and that he wanted to ask one question. Why had I not pocketed the two hundred rupees, and said nothing about it? My answer to this question was evidently satisfactory, for that evening, while waiting at the station in a state of uncertainty, I received two letters, one from Tewari thanking me for my contribution of two hundred rupees to the Railway men's Widows' and Orphans' Fund, of which he was Honorary Secretary, and the other from Izat informing me that my services were being retained, and instructing me to report to Ryles for duty.

For a year thereafter I worked up and down the railway on a variety of jobs, at times on the footplates of locomotives reporting on consumption of coal—a job I liked for I was permitted to drive the engines; at times as guard of goods trains, a tedious job, for the railway was short-handed and on many occasions I was on duty for forty-eight hours at a stretch; and at times as assistant storekeeper, or assistant station-master. And then one day I received orders to go to Mokameh Ghat and see Storrar, the Ferry Superintendent. The Bengal and North Western Railway runs through the Gangetic valley at varying distances from the Ganges river, and at several places branch lines take off from the main line and run down to the river and, by means of ferries, connect up with the broad gauge railways on the right bank. Mokameh Ghat on the right bank of the Ganges is the most important of these connexions.

I left Samastipur in the early hours of the morning and at the branch-line terminus, Samaria Ghat, boarded the S.S. Gorakhpur. Storrar had been apprised of my visit but no reason had been given, and as I had not been told why I was to go to Mokameh Ghat, we spent the day partly in his house and partly in walking about the extensive sheds, in which there appeared to be a considerable congestion of goods. Two days later I was summoned to Gorakhpur, the headquarters of the railway, and informed that I had been posted to Mokameh Ghat as Trans-shipment Inspector, that my pay had been increased from one hundred to one hundred and fifty rupees per month, and that I was to take over the contract for handling goods a week later.

So back to Mokameh Ghat I went, arriving on this occasion at night, to take up a job about which I knew nothing, and to take on a contract without knowing where to get a single labourer, and, most important of all, with a capital of only one hundred and fifty rupees, saved during my two and a half years' service.

Storrar was not expecting me on this occasion, but he gave me dinner, and when I told him why I had returned we took our chairs on to the veranda, where a cool wind was blowing off the river, and talked late into the night. Storrar was twice my age and had been at Mokameh Ghat for several years. He was employed as Ferry Superintendent by the Bengal and North Western (metre-gauge) Railway, and was in charge of a fleet of steamers and barges that ferried passengers and metre-gauge wagons between Samaria Ghat and Mokameh Ghat. I learnt from him that 80 per cent, of the long- distance traffic on the Bengal and North Western Railway passed through Mokameh Ghat; and that each year, from March to September, congestion of goods traffic took place at Mokameh Ghat and caused serious loss to the Railway.

The transfer of goods between the two railways at Mokameh Ghat, necessitated by a break of gauge, was done by a Labour Company which held the contract for handling goods throughout the length of the broad-gauge railway. In Storrar's opinion the indifference of this company to the interests of the metre-gauge railway, and the seasonal shortage of labour due to the harvesting of crops in the Gangetic valley, were the causes of the annual congestion. Having imparted this information, he very pertinently asked how I, a total stranger to the locality and without any capital—he brushed aside my hard-earned savings— proposed to accomplish what the Labour Company with all their resources had failed to do. The sheds at Mokameh Ghat, he added, were stacked to the roof with goods; there were four hundred wagons in the yard waiting to be unloaded, and a thousand wagons on the far side of the river waiting to be ferried across. 'My advice to you', he concluded, 'is to catch the early steamer to Samaria Ghat and to go straight back to Gorakhpur. Tell the Railway you will have nothing to do with the handling contract.'

I was up early next morning but I did not catch the steamer to Samaria Ghat. Instead, I went on a tour of inspection of the sheds and of the goods yard. Storrar had not over, painted the picture: in fact the conditions were even worse than he had said they were, for in addition to the four hundred metre-gauge wagons there were the same number of broad-gauge wagons waiting to be unloaded. At a rough calculation I put the goods at Mokameh Ghat waiting to be dealt with at fifteen thousand tons, and I had been sent to clear up the mess. Well, I was not quite twenty-one years of age, and summer was starting, a season when all of us are a little bit mad. By the time I met Ram Saran I had made up my mind that I would take on the job, no matter what the result might be. Ram Saran was station-master at Mokameh Ghat, a post he had held for two years. He was twenty years older than I was, had an enormous jet-black beard, and was the father of five children. He had been advised by telegram of my arrival, but had not been told that I was to take over the handling contract.

When I gave him this bit of news his face beamed all over and he said, 'Good, Sir. Very good. We will manage.' My heart warmed towards Ram Saran on hearing that 'we', and up to his death, thirty-five years later, it never cooled.

When I told Storrar over breakfast that morning that I had decided to take on the handling contract he remarked that fools never took good advice, but added that he would do all he could to help me, a promise he faithfully kept. In the months that followed he kept his ferry running day and night to keep me supplied with wagons.

The journey from Gorakhpur had taken two days, so

when I arrived at Mokameh Ghat I had five days in which to learn what my duties were, and to make arrangements for taking over the handling contract. The first two days I spent in getting acquainted with my staff which, in addition to Ram Saran, consisted of an assistant station-master, a grand old man by the name of Chatterji who was old enough to be my grandfather, sixty-five clerks, and a hundred shunters, pointsmen and watchmen. My duties extended across the river to Samaria Ghat where I had a clerical and menial staff a hundred strong. The supervising of these two staffs and the care of the goods in transit, was in itself a terrifying job and added to it was the responsibility of providing a labour force sufficient to keep the five hundred thousand tons of goods that passed through Mokameh Ghat annually, flowing smoothly.

The men employed by the big Labour Company were on piece work, and as all work at Mokameh Ghat was practically at a standstill, there were several hundred very discontented men sitting about the sheds, many of whom offered me their services when they heard that I was going to do the handling for the metre-gauge railway. I was under no agreement not to employ the Labour Company's men, but thought it prudent not to do so. However, I saw no reason why I should not employ their relatives, so on the first of the three days I had in hand I selected twelve men and appointed them headmen. Eleven of these headmen undertook to provide ten men each, to start with, for the handling of goods, and the twelfth undertook to provide a mixed gang of sixty men and women for the handling of coal. The traffic to be dealt with consisted of a variety of commodities, and this meant employing different castes to deal with the different classes of goods. So of the twelve headmen, eight were Hindus, two Mohammedans, and two men of the depressed class; and as only one of the twelve was literate I employed one Hindu and one Mohammedan clerk to keep their accounts.

While one Labour Company was doing the work of both railways the interchange of goods had taken place from wagon to wagon. Now each railway was to unload its goods in the sheds, and reload from shed to wagon. For all classes of goods, excluding heavy machinery and coal, I was to be paid at the rate of Re 1-7-0 (equivalent to 1s. lid. at the rate of exchange then current) for every thousand maunds of goods unloaded from wagons to shed or loaded from shed to wagons. Heavy machinery and coal were one-way traffic and as these two commodities were to be trans-shipped from wagon to wagon and only one contractor could be employed for the purpose, the work was entrusted to me, and I was to receive Re 1-4-0 (1s. 8d.) for unloading, and the same for loading, one thousand maunds. There are eighty pounds in a maund, and a thousand maunds therefore are equal to over thirty-five tons. These rates will appear incredible, but their accuracy can be verified by a reference to the records of the two railways.

A call-over on the last evening revealed that I had eleven headmen, each with a gang of ten men, and one headman with a mixed gang of sixty men and women. This, together with the two clerks, completed my force. At daybreak next morning I telegraphed to Gorakhpur that I had assumed my duties as Trans-shipment Inspector, and had taken over the handling contract.

Ram Saran's opposite number on the broad-gauge railway was an Irishman by the name of Tom Kelly. Kelly had been at Mokameh Ghat for some years and though he was very pessimistic of my success, he very sportingly offered to help me in every way he could. With the sheds congested with goods, and with four hundred wagons of each railway waiting to be unloaded, it was necessary to do something drastic to make room in the sheds and get the traffic moving, so I arranged with Kelly that I would take the risk of unloading a thousand tons of wheat on the ground outside the sheds and with the wagons so released clear a space in the sheds for Kelly to unload a thousand tons of salt and sugar. Kelly, then, with his empty wagons would clear a space in the sheds for me. This plan worked admirably. Fortunately for me it did not rain while my thousand tons of wheat were exposed to the weather, and in ten days we had not only cleared the accumulation in the sheds but also the accumulation of wagons. Kelly and I were then able to advise our respective headquarters to resume the booking of goods via Mokameh Ghat, which had been suspended for a fortnight.

I took over the contract at the beginning of the summer, the season when traffic on Indian railways is at its heaviest, and as soon as booking was opened a steady stream of downwards traffic from the Bengal and North Western Railway and an equally heavy stream from the broad-gauge railway started pouring into Mokameh Ghat. The rates on which I had been given the contract were the lowest paid to any contractor in India, and the only way in which I could hope to keep my labour was by cutting it down to the absolute minimum and making it work harder in order that it would earn as much, or possibly a little more, than other labour on similar work. All the labour at Mokameh Ghat was on piece work, and at the end of the first week my men and I were overjoyed to find that they had earned, on paper, 50 per cent more than the Labour Company's men had earned. When entrusting me with the contract the Railway promised to pay me weekly, and I on my part, promised to pay my labour weekly. The Railway, however, when making their promise, failed to realize that by switching over from one handling contractor to another they would be raising complications for their Audit Department that would take time to resolve. For the Railway this was a small matter, but for me it was very different. My total capital on arrival at Mokameh Ghat had been one hundred and fifty rupees, and there was no one in all the world I could call on to help me with a loan, so until the Railway paid me I could not pay my men.

I have entitled this story 'Loyalty' and I do not think that anyone has ever received greater loyalty than I did, not only from my labour, but also from the railway staff, during those first three months that I was at Mokameh Ghat. Nor do I think that men have ever worked harder. The work started every morning, weekdays and Sundays alike, at 4 a.m., and continued without interruption up to 8 p.m. The clerks whose duty it was to check and tally the goods took their meals at different hours to avoid a stoppage of work and my men ate their food, which was brought to them by wives, mothers, or daughters, in the sheds.

There were no trade unions or slaves and slave-drivers in those days and every individual was at liberty to work as many, or as few, hours as he or she wished to. And everyone worked cheerfully and happily; for no matter whether it was the procuring of more and better food and clothing for the family, the buying of a new ox to replace a worn-out one, or the paying-off of a debt, the incentive, without which no man can work his best, was there. My work and Ram Saran's did not end when the men knocked off work, for there was correspondence to attend to, and the next day's work to be planned and arranged for, and during those first three months neither of us spent more than four hours in bed each night. I was not twenty-one and as hard as nails, but Ram Saran was twenty years older and soft, and at the end of the three months he had lost a stone in weight but none of his cheerfulness.

Lack of money was now a constant worry to me, and as week succeeded week the worry became a hideous nightmare that never left me. First the headmen and then the labourers pledged their cheap and pitiful bits of jewellery and now all credit had gone; and to make matters worse, the men of the Labour Company, who were jealous that my men had earned more than they did, were beginning to taunt my men. On several occasions ugly incidents were narrowly avoided, for semi-starvation had not impaired the loyalty of my men and they were willing to give battle to anyone who as much as hinted that I had tricked them into working for me, and that they would never see a pice of the money they had earned. The monsoon was late in coming that year and the red ball in the sky, fanned by a wind from an unseen furnace, was making life a burden. At the end of a long and a very trying day I received a telegram from Samaria Ghat informing me that an engine had been derailed on the slipway that fed the barges on which wagons were ferried across to Mokameh Ghat. A launch conveyed me across the river and twice within the next three hours the engine was replaced on the track, with the aid of hand jacks, only to be derailed again. It was not until the wind had died down and the powdery sand could be packed under the wooden sleepers that the engine was re-railed for the third time, and the slipway again brought into use. Tired and worn out, and with eyes swollen and sore from the wind and sand, I had just sat down to my first meal that day when my twelve headmen filed into the room, and seeing my servant placing a plate in front of me, with the innate courtesy of Indians, filed out again. I then, as I ate my dinner, heard the following conversation taking place in the veranda.

One of the headmen. What was on the plate you put in front of the sahib?

My servant. A chapati and a little dal.

One of the headmen. Why only one chapati and a little dal?

My servant. Because there is no money to buy more. *One of the headmen.* What else does the sahib eat? *My servant.* Nothing.

After a short silence I heard the oldest of the headmen, a Mohammedan with a great beard dyed with henna, say to his companions, 'Go home. I will stay and speak to the sahib.'

When my servant had removed the empty plate the old headman requested permission to enter the room, and standing before me spoke as follows: 'We came to tell you that our stomachs have long been empty and that after tomorrow it would be no longer possible for us to work. But we have seen tonight that your case is as bad as ours and we will carry on as long as we have strength to stand. I will, with your permission, go now, sahib, and, for the sake of Allah, I beg you will do something to help us.'

Every day for weeks I had been appealing to headquarters at Gorakhpur for funds and the only reply I could elicit was that steps were being taken to make early payment of my bills. After the bearded headman left me that night I walked across to the Telegraph Office, where the telegraphist on duty was sending the report I submitted each night of the work done during the day, took a form off his table and told him to clear the line for an urgent message to Gorakhpur. It was then a few minutes after midnight and the message I sent read: 'Work at Mokameh Ghat ceases at midday today unless I am assured that twelve thousand rupees has been dispatched by morning train.' The telegraphist read the message over and looking up at me said: 'If I have your permission I will tell my brother, who is on duty at this hour, to deliver the message at once and not wait until office hours in the morning.' Ten hours later, and with two hours of my ultimatum still to run, I saw a telegraph messenger hurrying towards me with a buff-coloured envelope in his hand. Each group of men he passed stopped work to stare after him, for everyone in Mokameh Ghat knew the purport of the telegram I had sent at midnight.

After I had read the telegram the messenger, who was the son of my office peon, asked if the news was good; and when I told him it was good, he dashed off and his passage down the sheds was punctuated by shouts of delight. The money could not arrive until the following morning, but what did a few hours matter to those who had waited for long months?

The pay clerk who presented himself at my office next day, accompanied by some of my men carrying a cash chest slung on a bamboo pole and guarded by two policemen, was a jovial Hindu who was as broad as he was long and who exuded good humour and sweat in equal proportions. I never saw him without a pair of spectacles tied across his forehead with red tape. Having settled himself on the floor of my office he drew on a cord tied round his neck and from somewhere deep down in his person pulled up a key. He opened the cash chest, and lifted out twelve string-bags each containing one thousand freshly minted silver rupees. He licked a stamp, and stuck it to the receipt I had signed. Then, delving into a pocket that would comfortably have housed two rabbits, he produced an envelope containing bank notes to the value of four hundred and fifty rupees, my arrears of pay for three months.

I do not think anyone has ever had as great pleasure in paying out money as I had when I placed a bag containing a thousand rupees into the hands of each of the twelve headmen, nor do I think men have ever received money with greater pleasure than they did. The advent of the fat pay clerk had relieved a tension that had become almost unbearable, and the occasion called for some form of celebration, so the remainder of the day was declared a holiday—the first my men and I had indulged in for ninety- five days. I do not know how the others spent their hours of relaxation. For myself, I am not ashamed to admit that I spent mine in sound and restful sleep.

For twenty-one years my men and I worked the handling contract at Mokameh Ghat, and during the whole of that long period, and even when I was absent in France and in Waziristan during the 1914-18 war, the traffic flowed smoothly through the main outlet of the Bengal and North Western Railway with never a hitch. When we took over the contract, between four and five hundred thousand tons of goods were passing through Mokameh Ghat, and when I handed over to Ram Saran the traffic had increased to a million tons.

9

Budhu

Budhu was a man of the Depressed Class, and during all the years I knew him I never saw him smile: his life had been too hard and the iron had entered deep into his very soul. He was about thirty-five years of age, a tall, gaunt man, with a wife and two young children, when he applied to me for work. At his request I put him on to trans-shipping coal from broad-gauge trucks to metre-gauge wagons at Mokameh Ghat, for in this task men and women could work together, and Budhu wanted his wife to work with him.

The broad-gauge trucks and metre-gauge wagons stood opposite each other with a four-foot-wide sloping platform between, and the coal had to be partly shovelled and partly carried in baskets from the trucks into the wagons.

The work was cruelly hard, for there was no covering to the platform. In winter the men and women worked in bitter cold, often wet with rain for days on end, and in summer the brick platform and the iron floors of the trucks and wagons blistered their bare feet. A shovel in the hands of a novice, working for his bread and the bread of his children, is a cruel tool. The first day's work leaves the hands red and sore and the back with an ache that is a torment. On the second day blisters form on the hands, and the ache in the back becomes an even greater torment. On the third day the blisters break and become septic, and the back can, with difficulty, be straightened. Thereafter for a week or ten days only guts, and plenty of them, can keep the sufferer at work—as I know from experience.

Budhu and his wife went through all these phases, and often, when they had done sixteen hours' piece work and were dragging themselves to the quarters I had provided for them, I was tempted to tell them they had suffered enough and should look for other less strenuous work. But they were making good wages, better (Budhu said) than they had ever made before, so I let them carry on, and the day came when with hardened hands and backs that no longer ached they left their work with as brisk and as light a step as they had approached it.

I had some two hundred men and women trans-shipping coal at that time, for the coal traffic was as heavy as it always was in the summer. India was an exporting country in those days, and the wagons that took the grain, opium, indigo, hides and bones to Calcutta returned from the collieries in Bengal loaded with coal, five hundred thousand tons of which passed through Mokameh Ghat.

One day Budhu and his wife were absent from work. Dhamari, the headman of the coal gang, informed me that Budhu had received a postcard the previous day and had left that morning with his family, saying he would return to work as soon as it was possible for him to do so. Two months later the family returned and reoccupied their quarters, and Budhu and his wife worked as industriously as they had always done. At about the same time the following year Budhu, whose frame had now filled out, and his wife, who had lost her haggard look, again absented themselves from work. On this occasion they were absent three months, and looked tired and worn out on their return.

Except when consulted, or when information was voluntarily given, I never inquired into the private affairs of my work people, for Indians are sensitive on this point; so I did not know why Budhu periodically left his work which he invariably did after receiving a postcard. The post for the work people was delivered to the headmen and distributed by them to the men and women working under them, so I instructed Chamari to send Budhu to me the next time he received a card. Nine months later, when the coal traffic was unusually heavy and every man and woman in my employ was working to full capacity, Budhu, carrying a post card in his hand, presented himself at my office. The postcard was in a script that I could not read so I asked Budhu to read it to me. This he could not do, for he had not been taught to read and write, but he said Chamari had read it to him and that it was an order from his master to come at once as the crops were ready to harvest. The following was Budhu's story as he told it to me that day in my office, and his story is the story of millions of poor people in India.

'My grandfather, who was a field labourer, borrowed two rupees from the bania of the village in which he lived. The bania retained one of the rupees as advance interest for one year, and made my grandfather put his thumb-mark to an entry in his bhai khata (register of account). When my grandfather was able to do so from time to time, he paid the bania a few annas by way of interest. On the death of my grandfather my father took over the debt, which then amounted to fifty rupees. During my father's lifetime the debt increased to one hundred and fifteen rupees. In the meantime the old bania died and his son, who reigned in his place, sent for me when my father died and informed me that as the family debt now amounted to a considerable sum it would be necessary for me to give him a stamped and duly executed document. This I did, and as I had no money to pay for the stamped paper and for the registration of the document the bania advanced the required amount and added it to the debt, which together with interest now amounted to 130 rupees. As a special favour the bania consented to reduce the interest to 25 per cent. This favour he granted me on condition that my wife and I helped him each year to harvest his crops, until the debt was paid in full. This agreement, for my wife and I to work for the bania without wages, was written on another piece of paper to which I put my thumb-mark. For ten years my wife and I have helped to harvest the bania's crops, and each year after the bania has made up the account and entered it on the back of the stamped paper he takes my thumb impression on the document. I do not know how much the debt has increased since I took it over. For years I was not able to pay anything towards it, but since I have been working for you I have paid five, seven, and thirteen rupees—twenty-five rupees altogether.'

Budhu had never dreamed of repudiating the debt. To repudiate a debt was unthinkable: not only would it blacken his own face, but, what was far worse, it would blacken the reputation of his father and grandfather. So he continued to pay what he could in cash and in labour, and lived on without hope of ever liquidating the debt; on his death, it would be passed on to his eldest son.

Having elicited from Budhu the information that there was a Vakil in the village in which the bania lived, and taken his name and address, I told Budhu to return to work and said

I would see what could be done with the bania. Thereafter followed a long correspondence with an advocate, or lawyer. The Vakil, a stout-hearted Brahmin, who became a firm ally after the bania had insulted him by ordering him out of his house and telling him to mind his own business. From the Vakil I learnt that the bhai khata inherited by the bania from his father could not be produced in a court of law as evidence, for it bore the thumb-marks of men long since dead. The bania had tricked Budhu into executing a document which clearly stated that Budhu had borrowed 150 rupees at a rate of 25 per cent, interest. The Vakil advised me not to contest the case for the document Budhu had executed was valid, and Budhu had admitted its validity by paying three installments as part interest, and putting his thumb-mark to these payments on the document. When I had sent the Vakil a money order in full satisfaction of the debt, plus interest at 25 per cent, the bania surrendered the legal document, but he refused to surrender the private agreement binding Budhu and his wife to work without wages on harvesting his crops. It was only when I threatened, on the Vakil's advice, to prosecute for extortion that he handed the agreement over to the Vakil.

Budhu was very uneasy while these transactions were dragging on. He never spoke to me on the subject, but I could see from the way in which he looked at me whenever I passed him at work that he was speculating as to whether he had been wise in leaving me to deal with the all-powerful bania, and what his position would be if the bania suddenly appeared and demanded an explanation for his conduct. And then one day I received by registered post a heavily sealed letter containing a much thumb-marked legal document, an agreement also thumb-marked, a stamped receipt for the Vakil's fees, and a letter informing me that Budhu was now a free man. The whole transaction had cost me two hundred and twenty-five rupees.

Budhu was leaving work that evening when I met him, took the documents out of the envelope, and told him to hold them while I set a match to them. 'No, Sahib, no', he said.

'You must not burn these papers, for I am now your slave and, God willing, I will one day pay off my debt to you.'

Not only did Budhu never smile but he was also a very silent man. When I told him that, as he would not let me burn the papers, he could keep them, he only put his hands together and touched my feet; but when he raised his head and turned to walk away, tears were ploughing furrows down his coal-grimed face.

Only one of millions freed of a debt that had oppressed three generations, but had the number been legion, my pleasure could not have been greater, nor could any words have affected me more deeply than Budhu's mute gesture, and the tears that blinded him as he stumbled away to tell his wife that the bania's debt had been paid and that they were free.

10

Lala Jee

The passenger steamer was late in arriving from Samaria Ghat. I was standing on the landing stage, watching the passengers disembark and hurry up the ramp to the broad-gauge train, which I had arranged to detain a few minutes for them. Last to leave the steamer was a thin man with eyes sunk deep in their sockets, wearing a patched suit which in the days of long ago had been white, and carrying a small bundle tied up in a coloured handkerchief. By clutching the handrail of the gangway for support, he managed to gain the landing stage, but he turned off at the ramp, walked with slow and feeble steps to the edge of the river, and was violently and repeatedly sick. Having stooped to wash his face, he opened his bundle, took from it a sheet, spread it on the bank, and lay down with the Ganges water lapping the soles of his feet. Evidently he had no intention of catching the train, for when the warning bell rang and the engine whistled, he made no movement. He was lying on his back, and when I told him he had missed his train he opened his sunken eyes to look up at me and said, 'I have no need of trains, Sahib, for I am dying'.

It was the mango season, the hottest time of the year, when cholera is always at its worst. When the man passed me at the foot of the gangway I suspected he was suffering from cholera, and my suspicions were confirmed when I saw him being violently sick. In reply to my questions the man said he was travelling alone, and had no friends at Mokameh Ghat, so I helped him to his feet and led him the two hundred yards that separated my bungalow from the Ganges. Then I made him comfortable in my punkah coolie's house, which was empty, and detached from the servants' quarters.

I had been at Mokameh Ghat ten years, employing a large labour force. Some of the people lived under my supervision in houses provided by me, and the balance lived in surrounding villages. I had seen enough of cholera among my own people and also among the villagers to make me pray that if I ever contracted the hateful and foul disease, some Good Samaritan would take pity on me and put a bullet through my head, or give me an overdose of opium.

Few will agree with me that of the tens of thousands of people reported as having died of cholera each year at least half die not of cholera but of fear. We, who live in India, as distinct from those who visit the country for a longer or shorter period, are fatalists, believing that a man cannot die before his allotted time. This, however, does not mean that we are indifferent to epidemic diseases. Cholera is dreaded throughout the land, and when it comes in epidemic form as many die of stark fear as die of the actual disease.

There was no question that the man in my punkah coolie's house was suffering from a bad attack of cholera and if he was to survive, his faith and my crude treatment alone would pull him through, for the only medical aid within miles was a brute of a doctor, as callous as he was inefficient, and whose fat oily throat I am convinced I should have one day had the pleasure of cutting had not a young probationer clerk, who had been sent to me to train, found a less messy way of removing this medico who was hated by the whole staff. This young hopeful gained the confidence of the doctor and of his wife, both of whom were thoroughly immoral, and who confided to the clerk that they greatly missed the fleshpots of Egypt and the pleasures they had enjoyed before coming to Mokameh Ghat. This information set the clerk thinking, and a few nights later, and a little before the passenger steamer was due to leave for Samaria Ghat, a letter was delivered to the doctor, on reading which he told his wife that he had been summoned to Samaria Ghat to attend an urgent case and that he would be absent all night. He spruced himself up before leaving the house, was met outside by the clerk, and conducted in great secrecy to an empty room at the end of a block of buildings in which one of my pointsmen had died a few nights previously of coal-gas poisoning.

After the doctor had been waiting some time in the room, which had a single solid door and a small grated window, the door opened to admit a heavily veiled figure and was then pulled to and locked on the outside.

I was returning late that night through the goods sheds and overheard part of a very animated conversation between the probationer clerk and a companion he was relieving on night duty. Next morning on my way to work I saw a crowd of men in front of the late pointsman's quarters and was informed, by a most innocent-looking spectator, that there appeared to be someone inside, though the door was padlocked on the outside. I told my informant to get a hammer and break the lock off and hurried away on my lawful occasions, for I had no desire to witness the discomfiture, richly as it was deserved, of the man and his wife when the door was broken open. Three entries appear in my diary for that date: '(i) Doctor and his wife left on urgent private affairs. (2) Shiv Deb probationer confirmed as a Tally Clerk on salary of twenty rupees per month. (3) Lock, points, alleged to have been run over by engine, replaced by new one.' And that was the last Mokameh Ghat ever saw of the man who was a disgrace to the honourable profession he claimed to belong to.

I could not spare much time to nurse the thin man for I already had three cholera patients on my hands. From my servants I could expect no help, for they were of a different caste to the sufferer, and further, there was no justification for exposing them to the risk of infection. However, this did not matter, provided I could instil sufficient confidence into the man that my treatment was going to make him well. To this end I made it very clear to him that I had not brought him into my compound to die, and to give me the trouble of cremating him, but to make him well, and that it was only with his co-operation that this could be effected. That first night I feared that in spite of our joint efforts he would die, but towards morning he rallied and from then on his condition continued to improve and all that remained to be done was to build up his strength, which cholera drains out of the human body more quickly than any other disease. At the end of a week he was able to give me his story.

He was a Lala, a merchant, and at one time possessed a flourishing grain business; then he made the mistake of taking as partner a man about whom he knew nothing. For a few years the business prospered and all went well, but one day when he returned from a long journey he found the shop empty, and his partner gone. The little money in his possession was only sufficient to meet his personal debts, and bereft of credit he had to seek employment. This he found with a merchant with whom he had traded, and for ten years he had worked on seven rupees a month, which was only sufficient to support himself and his son—his wife having died shortly after his partner robbed him. He was on his way from Muzaffarpur to Gaya, on his master's business, when he was taken ill in the train. As he got worse on board the ferry steamer, he had crawled ashore to die on the banks of the sacred Ganges.

Lala Jee—I never knew him by any other name—stayed with me for about a month, and then one day he requested permission to continue his journey to Gaya. The request was made as we were walking through the sheds, for Lala Jee was strong enough now to accompany me for a short distance each morning when I set out for work, and when I asked him what he would do if on arrival at Gaya he found his master had filled his place, he said he would try to find other employment. 'Why not try to get someone to help you to be a merchant again?' I asked; and he replied: 'the thought of being a merchant once again, and able to educate my son, is with me night and day, Sahib, but there is no one in all the world who would trust me, a servant on seven rupees a month and without any security to offer, with the five hundred rupees I should need to give me a new start.'

The train for Gaya left at 8 p.m. and when that evening I returned to the bungalow a little before that hour, I found Lala Jee with freshly washed clothes, and a bundle in his hand a little bigger than the one he had arrived with, waiting in the veranda to say goodbye to me. When I put a ticket for Gaya and five one- hundred rupee notes into his hand he, like the man with the coal-grimed face, was tongue-tied. All he could do was to keep glancing from the notes in his hand to my face, until the bell that warned passengers the train would leave in five minutes, rang; then, putting his head on my feet, he said: 'Within one year your slave will return you this money.'

And so Lala Jee left me, taking with him the greater part of my savings. That I would see him again I never doubted, for the poor of India never forget a kindness; but the promise Lala Jee had made was, I felt sure, beyond his powers of accomplishment. In this I was wrong, for returning late one evening I saw a man dressed in spotless white standing in my veranda. The light from the room behind him was in my eyes, and I did not recognize him until he spoke. It was Lala Jee, come a few days before the expiry of the time limit he had set himself. That night as he sat on the floor near my chair he told me of his trading transactions, and the success that had attended them. Starting with a few bags of grain and being content with a profit of only four annas per bag he had gradually, and steadily, built up his business until he was able to deal in consignments up to thirty tons in weight, on which he was making a profit of three rupees per ton. His son was in a good school, and as he could now afford to keep a wife he had married the daughter of a rich merchant of Patna; all this he had accomplished in a little under twelve months. As the time drew near for his train to leave he laid five one-hundred rupee notes on my knee. Then, he took a bag from his pocket, held it out to me and said, 'this is the interest, calculated at 25 per cent, that I owe you on the money you lent me'. I believe I deprived him of half the pleasure he had anticipated from his visit when I told him it was not our custom to accept interest from our friends. Before leaving me Lala Jee said, 'during the month I stayed with you I had talks with your servants, and with your workmen, and I learnt from them that there was a time when you were reduced to one chapati and a little dal. If such a time should ever come again, which Parmeshwar forbid, your slave will place all that he has at your feet.'

Until I left Mokameh Ghat, eleven years later, I received each year a big basket of the choicest mangoes from Lala Jee's garden, for he attained his ambition of becoming a merchant once again, and returned to the home he had left when his partner robbed him.

11

Chamari

Chamari, as his name implies, belonged to the lowest strata of India's sixty million Untouchables. Accompanied by his wife, an angular person whose face was stamped with years of suffering and whose two young children were clutching her torn skirts, he applied to me for work. Chamari was an undersized man with a poor physique, and as he was not strong enough to work in the sheds I put him and his wife on to trans-shipping coal. Next morning I provided the pair of them with shovels and baskets, and they started work with courage and industry far beyond their strength. Towards evening I had to put others on to finishing their task, for the delay in unloading one of a rake of fifty wagons meant hanging up the work of several hundred labourers.

For two days Chamari and his wife laboured valiantly but ineffectively. On the third morning when, their blistered hands tied up in dirty rags, they were waiting for work to be allotted to them I asked Chamari if he could read and write. When he said that he knew a little Hindi, I instructed him to return the shovels and baskets to the store and to come to my office for orders. A few days previously I had discharged the headman of the coal gang for his inability to keep sober—the only man I ever discharged—and as it was quite evident that neither Chamari nor his wife would be able to make a living at the job they were on, I decided to give Chamari a trial as a headman.

Chamari thought he had been summoned to the office to be sacked and was greatly relieved, and very proud, when I handed him a new account book and a pencil and told him to take down the numbers of the rake of broad-gauge wagons from which coal was being unloaded, together with the names of the men and women who were engaged on each wagon. Half an hour later he returned with the information I had asked for, neatly entered in the book. When I had verified the correctness of these entries I handed the book back to Chamari, told him I had appointed him headman of the coal gang, at that time numbering two hundred men and women, and explained his duties to him in detail. A humble man, who, one short hour earlier had laboured under all the disqualifications of his lowly birth walked out of my office with a book tucked under his arm, a pencil behind his ear and, for the first time in his life, his head in the air.

Chamari was one of the most conscientious and hardworking men I have ever employed. In the gang he commanded, there were men and women of all castes including Brahmins, Chattris and Thakurs, and never once did he offend by rendering less respect to these high-caste men and women than was theirs by birthright, and never once was his authority questioned. He was responsible for keeping the individual accounts of everyone working under him and during the twenty years he worked for me the correctness of his accounts was never disputed.

On Sunday evenings Chamari and I would sit, he on a mat and I on a stool, with a great pile of copper pice between us, and ringed round by coal-grimed men and women eagerly waiting for their week's wages. I enjoyed those Sunday evenings as much as did the simple hardworking people sitting round me, for my pleasure in giving them the wages they had earned with the sweat of their brows was as great as theirs in receiving them.

During the week they worked on a platform half a mile long, and as some of them lived in the quarters I had built for them, while others lived in the surrounding villages, they had little opportunity for social intercourse. Sunday evenings gave them this opportunity, and they took full advantage of it. Hardworking people are always cheerful, for they have no time to manufacture imaginary troubles, which are always worse than real ones. My people were admittedly poor, and they had their full share of troubles; none the less they were full of good cheer, and as I could understand and speak their language as well as they could, I was able to take part in their light-hearted banter and appreciate all their jokes.

The railway paid me by weight and I paid my people, both those who worked in the sheds and those who worked on the coal platform, at wagon rates. For work in the sheds I paid the headmen, who in turn paid the gangs employed by them, but the men and women working on coal were paid individually by me. Chamari would change the currency notes I gave him for pice in the Mokameh bazaar, and then, on Sunday evenings, as we sat with the pile of pice between us he would read out the names of the men and women who had been engaged on unloading every individual wagon during the week, while I made a quick mental calculation and paid the amount due to each worker. I paid forty pice (ten annas) for the unloading of each wagon, and when the pice would not divide up equally among the number that had been engaged on unloading any particular wagon I gave the extra pice to one of their number, who would later purchase salt to be divided among them. This system of payment worked to the satisfaction of everyone, and though the work was hard, and the hours long, the wage earned was three times as much as could be earned on field work, and further, my work was permanent while field work was seasonal and temporary.

I started Chamari on a salary of fifteen rupees a month and gradually increased it to forty rupees, which was more than the majority of the clerks employed by the railway were getting, and in addition I allowed him to employ a gang of ten men to work in the sheds. In India a man's worth is assessed, to a great extent, by the money he is earning and the use he makes of it. Chamari was held in great respect by all sections of the community for the good wages he was earning, but he was held in even greater respect for the unobtrusive use he made of his money. Having known hunger, he made it his business to see that no one whom he could succor, suffered as he had suffered. All of his own lowly caste who passed his door were welcome to share his food, and those whose caste prohibited them from eating the food cooked by his wife were provided with material to enable them to prepare their own food. When at his wife's request I spoke to Chamari on the subject of keeping open house, his answer invariably was that he and his family had found the fifteen rupees per month, on which I had engaged him, sufficient for their personal requirements and that to allow his wife more than that sum now would only encourage her to be extravagant. When I asked what form her extravagance was likely to take, he said she was always nagging him about his clothes and telling him he should be better dressed than the men who were working under him, whereas he thought money spent on clothes could be better spent on feeding the poor. Then to clinch the argument he said: 'Look at yourself, Maharaj,'—he had addressed me thus from the first day, and continued so to address me to the end—'you have been wearing that suit for years, and if you can do that, why can't I?' As a matter of fact he was wrong about the suit, for I had two of the same material, one being cleaned of coal dust while the other was in use.

I had been at Mokameh Ghat sixteen years when Kaiser Wilhelm started his war. The railway opposed my joining up but gave their consent when I agreed to retain the contract. It was impossible to explain the implications of the war to my people at the conference to which I summoned them. However, each and every one of them was willing to carry on during my absence, and it was entirely due to their loyalty and devotion that traffic through Mokameh Ghat flowed smoothly and without a single hitch during the years I was serving, first in France, and later in Waziristan. Ram Saran acted as Trans-shipment Inspector during my absence, and when I returned after four years I resumed contact with my people with the pleasant feeling that I had only been away from them for a day. My safe return was attributed by them to the prayers they had offered up for me in temples, and mosques, and at private shrines.

The summer after my return from the war cholera was bad throughout Bengal, and at one time two women and a man of the coal gang were stricken down by the disease. Chamari and I nursed the sufferers by turns, instilling confidence into them, and by sheer will power brought them through. Shortly thereafter I heard someone moving in my veranda one night—I had the bungalow to myself, for Storrar had left on promotion—and on my asking, who it was, a voice out of the darkness said, 'I am Chamari's wife. I have come to tell you that he has cholera'. Telling the woman to wait, I hastily donned some clothes, lit a lantern and set off with her armed with a stick, for Mokameh Ghat was infested with poisonous snakes.

Chamari had been at work all that day and in the afternoon had accompanied me to a nearby village in which a woman of his coal gang, by the name of Parbatti, was reported to be seriously ill. Parbatti, a widow with three children, was the first woman to volunteer to work for me when I arrived at Mokameh Ghat and for twenty years she had worked unflaggingly. Always cheerful and happy and willing to give a helping hand to any who needed it, she was the life and soul of the Sunday evening gatherings, for, being a widow, she could bandy words with all and sundry without offending India's very strict Mother Grundy.

The boy who brought me the news that she was ill did not know what ailed her, but was convinced that she was dying, so I armed myself with a few simple remedies and calling for Chamari on the way, hurried to the village. We found Parbatti lying on the floor of her hut with her head in her grey-haired mother's lap. It was the first case of tetanus I had ever seen, and I hope the last I shall ever see. Parbatti's teeth, which would have made the fortune of a film star, had been broken in an attempt to lever them apart, to give her water. She was conscious, but unable to speak, and the torments she was enduring are beyond any words of mine to describe. There was nothing I could do to give her relief beyond massaging the tense muscles of her throat to try to ease her breathing, and while I was doing this, her body was convulsed as though she had received an electric shock. Mercifully her heart stopped beating, and her sufferings ended. Chamari and I had no words to exchange as we walked away from the humble home in which preparations were already under way for the cremation ceremony, for though an ocean of prejudices had lain between the high-caste woman and us, it had made no difference to our affection for her, and we both knew that we would miss the cheerful, hardworking little woman more than either of us cared to admit. I had not seen Chamari again that evening, for work had taken me to Samaria Ghat, and now his wife had come to tell me he was suffering from cholera.

We in India loathe and dread cholera but we are not frightened of infection, possibly because we are fatalists, and I was not surprised therefore to find a number of men squatting on the floor round Chamari's string bed. The room was dark, but he recognized me in the light of the lantern I was carrying and said, 'Forgive the woman for having called you at this hour.'—it was 2 a.m.—'I ordered her not to disturb you until morning and she disobeyed me.' Chamari had left me, apparently in good health, ten hours previously and I was shocked to see the change those few hours had made in his appearance. Always a thin, lightly built man, he appeared to have shrunk to half his size; his eyes had sunk deep into their sockets, and his voice was weak and little more than a whisper. It was oppressively hot in the room, so I covered his partly naked body with a sheet and made the men carry the bed out into the open courtyard. It was a public place for a man suffering from cholera to be in, but better a public place than a hot room in which there was not sufficient air for a man in his condition to breathe.

Chamari and I had fought many cases of cholera together

and he knew, none better, the danger of panicking and the necessity for unbounded faith in the simple remedies at my command. Heroically he fought the foul disease, never losing hope and taking everything I offered him to combat the cholera and sustain his strength. Hot as it was, he was cold, and the only way I was able to maintain any heat in his body was by placing a brazier with hot embers under his bed, and getting helpers to rub powdered ginger into the palms of his hands and the soles of his feet. For forty-eight hours the battle lasted, every minute being desperately contested with death, and then the gallant little man fell into a coma, his pulse fading out and his breathing becoming hardly perceptible. From midnight to a little after 4 a.m. he lay in this condition, and I knew that my friend would never rally. Hushed people who had watched with me during those long hours were either sitting on the ground or standing round when Chamari suddenly sat up and in an urgent and perfectly natural voice said, 'Maharaj, Maharaj! Where are you?' I was standing at the head of the bed, and when I leant forward and put my hand on his shoulder he caught it in both of his and said, 'Maharaj, Parmeshwar is calling me, and I must go'. Then, putting his hands together and bowing his head, he said, 'Parmeshwar, I come'. He was dead when I laid him back on the bed.

Possibly a hundred people of all castes were present and heard Chamari's last words, and among them was a stranger, with sandalwood caste-marks on his forehead. When I laid the wasted frame down on the bed, the stranger asked who the dead man was and, when told that he was Chamari, said:

'I have found what I have long been searching for. I am a priest of the great Vishnu temple at Kashi. My master the head priest, hearing of the good deeds of this man, sent me to find him and take him to the temple that he might have darshan of him. And now I will go back to my master and tell him Chamari is dead, and I will repeat to him the words I heard Chamari say.' Then, having laid the bundle he was carrying on the ground, and slipped off his sandals, this Brahmin priest approached the foot of the bed and made obeisance to the dead Untouchable.

There will never again be a funeral like Chamari's at Mokameh Ghat, for all sections of the community, high and low, rich and poor, Hindu, Mohammedan, Untouchable and Christian, turned out to pay their last respects to one who had arrived friendless and weighed down with disqualifications, and who left respected by all and loved by many. Chamari was a heathen, according to our Christian belief, and the lowest of India's Untouchables, but if I am privileged to go where he has gone, I shall be content.

12

Life at Mokameh Ghat

My men and I did not spend all our time at Mokameh Ghat working and sleeping. Work at the start had been very strenuous for all of us, and continued to be so, but as time passed and hands hardened and back-muscles developed, we settled down in our collars, and as we were pulling in the same direction with a common object—better conditions for those dependent on us—work moved smoothly and allowed of short periods for recreation. The reputation we had earned for ourselves by clearing the heavy accumulation of goods at Mokameh Ghat, and thereafter keeping the traffic moving, was something that all of us had contributed towards, and all of us took a pride in having earned this reputation and were determined to retain it. When, therefore, an individual absented himself to attend to private affairs, his work was cheerfully performed by his companions.

One of my first undertakings, when I had a little time to myself and a few rupees in my pocket, was to start a school for the sons of my workmen, and for the sons of the lower paid railway staff. The idea originated with Ram Saran, who was a keen educationist, possibly because of the few opportunities he himself had had for education. Between us, we rented a hut, installed a master, and the school—known ever afterwards as Ram Saran's School—started with a membership of twenty boys. Caste prejudices were the first snag we ran up against, but our master soon circumnavigated it by removing the sides of the hut. For whereas high- and low-caste boys could not sit together in cold brittle air in the same hut, there was no objection to their sitting in the same shed. From the very start, the school was a great success, thanks entirely to Ram Saran's unflagging interest. When suitable buildings had been erected, an additional seven masters employed, and the students increased to two hundred, the Government relieved us of our financial responsibilities. They raised the school to the status of a Middle School and rewarded Ram Saran, to the delight of all his friends, by conferring on him the title of Rai Sahib.

Tom Kelly, Ram Saran's opposite number on the broad-gauge railway, was a keen sportsman, and he and I started a recreation club. We cleared a plot of ground, marked out a football and a hockey ground, erected goal-posts, purchased a football and hockey sticks, and started to train each his own football and hockey team. The training for football was comparatively easy, but not so the training for hockey, for as our means did not run to the regulation hockey stick we purchased what at that time was known as a Khalsa stick: this was made in Punjab from a blackthorn or small oak tree, the root being bent to a suitable angle to form the crook. The casualties at the start were considerable, for 98 per cent, of the players were bare footed, the sticks were heavy and devoid of lapping and the ball used was made of wood. When our teams had learnt the rudiments of the two games, which amounted to no more than knowing in which direction to propel the ball, we started inter-railway matches.

The matches were enjoyed as much by the spectators as by us who took part in them. Kelly was stouter than he would have admitted to being and always played in goal for his side, or for our team when we combined to play out-station teams.

I was thin and light and played centre forward and was greatly embarrassed when I was accidentally tripped up by foot or by hockey stick, for when this happened, all the players, with the exception of Kelly, abandoned the game to set me on my feet and dust my clothes. On one occasion while I was receiving these attentions, one of the opposing team dribbled the ball down the field and was prevented from scoring a goal by the spectators, who impounded the ball and arrested the player!

Shortly after we started the recreation club, the Bengal and North Western Railway built a club house and made a tennis court for their European staff which, including myself, numbered four. Kelly was made an honorary member of the club, and a very useful member he proved, for he was good at both billiards and tennis. Kelly and I were not able to indulge in tennis more than two or three times a month, but when the day's work was done we spent many pleasant evenings together playing billiards.

The goods sheds and sidings at Mokameh Ghat were over a mile and a half long, and to save Kelly unnecessary walking, his railway provided him with a rail trolly and four men to push it. This trolly was a great joy to Kelly and myself, for during the winter months, when the barheaded and greylag geese were in, and the moon was at or near the full, we trolled down the main line for nine miles to where there were a number of small tanks. These tanks, some of which were only a few yards across while others were an acre or more in extent, were surrounded by lentil crops which gave us ample cover. We timed ourselves to arrive at the tanks as the sun was setting, and shortly after we had taken up our positions—Kelly at one of the tanks and I at another—we would see the geese coming.

The geese, literally tens of thousands of them, spent the day on the islands in the Ganges and in the evening, left the islands to feed on the weeds in the tanks, or on the ripening wheat and grain crops beyond. After crossing the railway line, which was half-way between our positions and the Ganges, the geese would start losing height, and they passed over our heads within easy range. Shooting by moonlight needs a little practice, for birds flighting overhead appear to be farther off than they actually are and one is apt to fire too far ahead of them. When this happened, the birds, seeing the flash of the gun and hearing the report, sprang straight up in the air and before they flattened out, again were out of range of the second barrel. Those winter evenings when the full moon was rising over the palm-trees that fringed the river, and the cold brittle air throbbed and reverberated with the honking of geese and the swish of their wings as they passed overhead in flights of ten to a hundred, are among the happiest of my recollections of the years I spent at Mokameh Ghat.

My work was never dull, and time never hung heavy on my hands, for in addition to arranging for the crossing of the Ganges, and the handling at Mokameh Ghat of a million tons of goods, I was responsible for the running of the steamers that ferried several hundred thousand passengers annually between the two banks of the river. The crossing of the river, which after heavy rains in the Himalayas was four to five miles wide, was always a pleasure to me, not only because it gave me time to rest my legs and have a quiet smoke but also because it gave me an opportunity of indulging in one of my hobbies—the study of human beings. The ferry was a link between two great systems of railways, one radiating north and the other radiating south, and among the seven hundred passengers who crossed at each trip were people from all parts of India, and from countries beyond her borders.

One morning I was leaning over the upper deck of the steamer watching the third-class passengers taking their seats on the lower deck. With me was a young man from England who had recently joined the railway, and who had been sent to me to study the system of work at Mokameh Ghat. He had spent a fortnight with me and I was now accompanying him across the river to Samaria Ghat to see him off on his long railway journey to Gorakhpur. Sitting cross-legged, or tailor wise, on a bench next to me and also looking down on the lower deck was an Indian. Crosthwaite, my young companion, was very enthusiastic about everything in the country in which he had come to serve, and as we watched the chattering crowds accommodating themselves on the open deck, he remarked that he would dearly love to know who these people were, and why they were travelling from one part of India to another. The crowd, packed like sardines, had now settled down, so I said I would try to satisfy his curiosity. Let us start, I said, at the right and work round the deck, taking only the outer fringe of people who have their backs to the rail. The three men nearest to us are Brahmins, and the big copper vessels, sealed with wet clay, that they are so carefully guarding, contain Ganges water. The water on the right bank of the Ganges is considered to be more holy than the water on the left bank and these three Brahmins, servants of a well-known Maharaja, have filled the vessels on the right bank and are taking the water eighty miles by river and rail for the personal use of the Maharaja who, even when he is travelling, never uses any but Ganges water for domestic purposes. The man next to the Brahmins is a Mohammedan, a dhoonia by profession. He travels from station to station teasing the cotton in old and lumpy mattresses with the harp-like implement lying on the deck beside him. With this implement he teases old cotton until it resembles floss silk. Next to him are two Tibetan lamas who are returning from a pilgrimage to the sacred Buddhist shrine at Gaya, and who, even on this winter morning, are feeling hot, as you can see from the beads of sweat standing out on their foreheads. Next to the lamas are a group of four men returning from a pilgrimage to Benares, to their home on the foothills of Nepal. Each of the four men, as you can see, has two blown- glass jars, protected with wickerwork, slung to a short bamboo pole. These jars contain water which they have drawn from the Ganges at Benares and which they will sell drop by drop in their own and adjoining villages for religious ceremonies.

And so, on round the deck, until I came to the last man on the left. This man, I told Crosthwaite, was an old friend of mine, the father of one of my workmen, who was crossing the river to plough his field on the left bank.

Crosthwaite listened with great interest to all I had told him about the passengers on the lower deck, and he now asked me who the man was who was sitting on the bench near us.

'Oh', I said, 'he is a Mohammedan gentleman. A hide merchant on his way from Gaya to Muzaffarpur.' As I ceased speaking the man on the bench unfolded his legs, placed his feet on the deck and started laughing. Then turning tome he said in perfect English, 'I have been greatly entertained listening to the description you have given your friend of the men on the deck below us, and also of your description of me.' My tan hid my blushes, for I had assumed that he did not know English. 'I believe that with one exception, myself, your descriptions were right in every case. I am a Mohammedan as you say, and I am travelling from Gaya to Muzaffarpur, though how you know this I cannot think for I have not shown my railway ticket to anyone since I purchased it at Gaya. But you were wrong in describing me as a hide merchant. I do not deal in hides. I deal in tobacco.'

On occasions, special trains were run for important personages, and in connexion with these trains a special ferry steamer was run, for the timings of which I was responsible. I met one afternoon one of these special trains, which was conveying the Prime Minister of Nepal, twenty ladies of his household, a Secretary, and a large retinue of servants from Katmandu, the capital of Nepal, to Calcutta. As the train came to a standstill, a blond-headed giant in Nepalese national dress jumped down from the train and went to the carriage in which the Prime Minister was travelling. Here the man opened a big umbrella, put his back to the door of the carriage, lifted his right arm and placed his hand on his hip. Presently the door behind him opened and the Prime Minister appeared, carrying a gold-headed cane in his hand. With practiced ease the Prime Minister took his seat on the man's arm and when he had made himself comfortable the man raised the umbrella over the Prime Minister's head and set off. He carried his burden as effortlessly as another would have carried a celluloid doll on his three-hundred-yard walk, over loose sand, to the steamer. When I remarked to the Secretary, with whom I was acquainted, that I had never seen a greater feat of strength, he informed me that the Prime Minister always used the blond giant in the way I had just seen him being used, when other means of transport were not available. I was told that the man was a Nepalese, but my guess was that he was a national of northern Europe who for reasons best known to himself, or to his masters, had accepted service in an independent state on the borders of India.

While the Prime Minister was being conveyed to the steamer, four attendants produced a rectangular piece of black silk, some twelve feet long and eight feet wide, which they laid on the sand close to a carriage, which had all its windows closed. The rectangle was fitted with loops at the four corners, and when hooks at the ends of four eight-foot silver staves had been inserted into the loops, and the staves stood on end, the rectangle revealed itself as a box-like structure without a bottom. One end of this structure was now raised to the level of the door of the closed carriage, and out of the carriage and into the silk box, stepped the twenty ladies of the Prime Minister's household. With the stave- bearers walking on the outside of the box and only the twinkling patent-leather-shod feet of the ladies showing, the procession set off for the steamer. On the lower deck of the steamer, one end of the box was raised and the ladies, all of whom appeared to be between sixteen and eighteen years of age, ran lightly up the stairway on to the upper deck, where I was talking to the Prime Minister. On a previous occasion I had suggested leaving the upper deck when the ladies arrived and had been told there was no necessity for me to do so and that the silk box was only intended to prevent the common men from seeing the ladies of the household. It is not possible for me to describe in detail the dress of the ladies, and all I can say is that in their gaily coloured, tight- fitting bodices and wide-spreading trousers, in the making of each of which forty yards of fine silk had been used, they looked, as they flitted from side to side of the steamer in an effort to see all that was to be seen, like rare and gorgeous butterflies. At Mokameh Ghat the same procedure was adopted to convey the Prime Minister and his ladies from the steamer to their special train, and when the whole party and their mountain of luggage were on board, the train steamed off on its way to Calcutta. Ten days later the party returned and I saw them off at Samaria Ghat on their way to Katmandu.

A few days later I was working on a report that had to go in that night when my friend, the Secretary, walked into my office. With his clothes dirty and creased, and looking as though they had been slept in for many nights, he presented a very different appearance from the spruced and well-dressed official I had last seen in company with the Prime Minister. He accepted the chair I offered him and said, without any preamble, that he was in great trouble. The following is the story he told me.

'On the last day of our visit to Calcutta, the Prime Minister took the ladies of his household to the shop of Hamilton and Co., the leading jewellers in the city, and told them to select the jewels they fancied. The jewels were paid for in silver rupees for, as you know, we always take sufficient cash with us from Nepal to pay all our expenses and for everything we purchase. The selection of the jewels, the counting of the cash, the packing of the jewels into the suitcase I had taken to the shop for the purpose, and the sealing of the case by the jeweller, all took more time than we had anticipated. The result was that we had to dash back to our hotel, collect our luggage and retinue and hurry to the station where our special train was waiting for us.

'We arrived back in Katmandu in the late evening, and the following morning the Prime Minister sent for me and asked for the suitcase containing the jewels. Every room in the palace was searched and everyone who had been on the trip to Calcutta was questioned, yet no trace of the suitcase was found, nor would anyone admit having seen it at any time. I remembered having taken it out of the motor-car that conveyed me from the shop to the hotel, but thereafter I could not remember having seen it at any stage of the journey. I am personally responsible for the case and its contents and if it is not recovered I may lose more than my job, for according to the laws of our land I have committed a great crime.

'there is in Nepal a hermit who is credited with second sight, and on the advice of my friends I went to him. I found the hermit, an old man in tattered clothing, living in a cave on the side of a great mountain, and to him I told my troubles. He listened to me in silence, asked no questions, and told me to return next morning. The following morning I again visited him and he told me that as he lay asleep the previous night he had a vision. In the vision he had seen the suitcase, with its seals intact, in a corner of a room hidden under boxes and bags of many kinds. The room was not far from a big river, had only one door leading into it, and this door was facing the east. This is all the hermit could tell me, so', the Secretary concluded, with tears in his eyes and a catch in his throat, 'I obtained permission to leave Nepal for a week and I have come to see if you can help me, for it is possible that the Ganges is the river the hermit saw in his vision.'

In the Himalayas no one doubts the ability of individuals

alleged to be gifted with second sight to help in recovering property lost or mislaid. That the Secretary believed what the hermit had told him, there was no question, and his anxiety now was to regain possession of the suitcase, containing jewellery valued at Rs.150,000 (£10,000), before others found and rifled it.

There were many rooms at Mokameh Ghat in which a miscellaneous assortment of goods was stored, but none of them answered to the description given by the hermit. I did, however, know of one room that answered to the description, and this room was the parcel office at Mokameh Junction, two miles from Mokameh Ghat. Having borrowed Kelly's trolly, I sent the Secretary to the Junction with Ram Saran. At the parcel office the clerk in charge denied all knowledge of the suitcase, but he raised no objection to the pile of luggage in the office being taken out on to the platform, and when this had been done, the suitcase was revealed with all its seals intact.

The question then arose as to how the case came to be in the office without the clerk's knowledge. The station master now came on the scene and his inquiries elicited the fact that the suitcase had been put in the office by a carriage sweeper, the lowest-paid man on the staff. This man had been ordered to sweep out the train in which the Prime Minister had travelled from Calcutta to Mokameh Ghat, and tucked away under the seat in one of the carriages he had found the suitcase. When his task was finished he carried the suitcase a distance of a quarter of a mile to the platform, and there being no one on the platform at the time to whom he could hand over the case he had put it in a corner of the parcel office. He expressed regret, and asked for forgiveness if he had done anything wrong.

Bachelors and their servants, as a rule, get into more or less set habits and my servants and I were no exception to the rule. Except when work was heavy I invariably returned to my house at 8 p.m. and when my house servant, waiting on the veranda, saw me coming he called to the waterman to lay my bath, for whether it was summer or winter I always had a hot bath. There were three rooms at the front of the house opening on to the veranda: a dining room, a sitting room and a bedroom. Attached to the bedroom was a small bathroom, ten feet long, and six, wide. This bathroom had two doors and one small window. One of the doors opened on to the veranda, and the other led to the bedroom. The window was opposite the bedroom door, and set high up in the outer wall of the house. The furniture of the bathroom consisted of an egg-shaped wooden bath, long enough to sit in, a wooden bath-mat with holes in it, and two earthen vessels containing cold water. After the waterman had laid the bath, my servant would bolt the outer door of the bathroom and on his way through the bedroom, pick up the shoes I had discarded and take them to the kitchen to clean. There he would remain until I called for dinner.

One night after my servant had gone to the kitchen I took a small hand-lamp off the dressing table, went into the bathroom and there placed it on a low wall, six inches high and nine inches wide, which ran half-way across- the width of the room. Then I turned and bolted the door, which like most doors in India sagged on its hinges and would not remain shut unless bolted. I had spent most of that day on the coal platform so did not spare the soap, and with a lather on my head and face that did credit to the manufacturers, I opened my eyes to replace the soap on the bath-mat and, to my horror, saw the head of a snake projecting up over the end of the bath and within a few inches of my toes. My movements while soaping my head and splashing the water about had evidently annoyed the snake, a big cobra, for its hood was expanded and its long forked tongue was flicking in and out of its wicked-looking mouth. The right thing for me to have done would have been to keep my hands moving, draw my feet away from the snake, and moving very slowly stand up and step backwards to the door behind me, keeping my eyes on the snake all the time. But what I very foolishly did was to grab the sides of the bath and stand up and step backwards, all in one movement, on to the low wall. On this cemented wall my foot slipped, and while trying to regain my balance a stream of water ran off my elbow on to the wick of the lamp and extinguished it, plunging the room in pitch darkness. So here I was, shut in a small dark room with one of the most deadly snakes in India. One step to the left or one step to the rear would have taken me to either of the two doors, but not knowing where the snake was, I was frightened to move for fear of putting my bare foot on it. Moreover, both doors were bolted at the bottom, and even if I avoided stepping on the snake I should have to feel about for the bolts where the snake, in his efforts to get out of the room, was most likely to be.

The servants' quarters were in a corner of the compound fifty yards away on the dining-room side of the house, so shouting to them would be of no avail, and my only hope of rescue was that my servant would get tired of waiting for me to call for dinner, or that a friend would come to see me, and I devoutly hoped this would happen before the cobra bit me. The fact that the cobra was as much trapped as I was, in no way comforted me, for only a few days previously one of my men had had a similar experience. He had gone into his house in the early afternoon in order to put away the wages I had just paid him. While he was opening his box he heard a hiss behind him, and turning round, saw a cobra advancing towards him from the direction of the open door. Backing against the wall behind him, for there was only one door to the room, the unfortunate man had tried to fend off the cobra with his hands, and while doing so was bitten twelve times on hands and on legs. Neighbours heard his cries and came to his rescue, but he died a few minutes later.

I learnt that night that small things can be more nerve-racking and terrifying than big happenings. Every drop of water that trickled down my legs was converted in my imagination into the long forked tongue of the cobra licking my bare skin, a prelude to the burying of his fangs in my flesh.

How long I remained in the room with the cobra I cannot say. My servant said later that it was only half an hour, and no sound has ever been more welcome to me than the sounds I heard as my servant laid the table for dinner. I called him to open the bathroom door, told him of my predicament and instructed him to fetch a lantern and a ladder. After another long wait I heard a babel of voices, followed by the scraping of the ladder against the outer wall of the house. When the lantern had been lifted to the window, ten feet above ground, it did not illuminate the room, so I told the man who was holding it to break a pane of glass and pass the lantern through the opening. The opening was too small for the lantern to be passed in upright. However, after it had been relit three times it was finally inserted into the room and, feeling that the cobra was behind me, I turned my head and saw it lying at the bottom of the bedroom door two feet away. Leaning forward very slowly, I picked up the heavy bath-mat, raised it high and let it fall as the cobra was sliding over the floor towards me. Fortunately I judged my aim accurately and the bath mat crashed down on the cobra's neck six inches from its head. As it bit at the wood and lashed about with its tail, I took a hasty stride to the veranda door and in a moment, was outside among a crowd of men, armed with sticks and carrying lanterns, for word had got round to the railway quarters that I was having a life-and-death struggle with a big snake in a locked room.

The pinned-down snake was soon dispatched and it was not until the last of the men had gone, leaving their congratulations, that I realized I had no clothes on and that my eyes were full of soap. How the snake came to be in the bathroom I never knew. It may have entered by one of the doors, or it may have fallen from the roof, which was made of thatch and full of rats and squirrels, and tunnelled with sparrows' nests. Anyway, the servants, who had laid my bath and I, had much to be thankful for, for we approached that night very near the gate of the Happy Hunting Grounds.

We at Mokameh Ghat observed no Hindu or Mohammedan holidays, for no matter what the day was work had to go on. There was, however, one day in the year that all of us looked forward to with anticipation and great pleasure, and that day was Christmas. On this day, custom ordained that I should remain in my house until ten o'clock, and punctually at this hour, Ram Saran—dressed in his best clothes and wearing an enormous pink silk turban, specially kept for the occasion— would present himself to conduct me to my office. Our funds did not run to bunting, but we had a large stock of red and green signal flags, and with these flags and strings of marigold and jasmine flowers, Ram Saran and his band of willing helpers, working from early morning, had given the office and its surroundings a gay and festive appearance. Near the office door a table and a chair were set, and on the table stood a metal pot containing a bunch of my best roses tied round with twine, as tight as twine could be tied. Ranged in front of the table were the railway staff, my headmen and all my labourers. And all were dressed in clean clothes, for no matter how dirty we were during the rest of the year, on Christmas Day we had to be clean.

After I had taken my seat on the chair and Ram Saran had put a garland of jasmine round my neck, the proceedings started with a long speech by Ram Saran, followed by a short one by me. Sweets were then distributed to the children, and after this messy proceeding was over to the satisfaction of all concerned, the real business of the day started—the distribution of a cash bonus to Ram Saran, to the staff and to the labourers. The rates I received for my handling contract were woefully small, but even so, by the willing co-operation of all concerned, I did make a profit, and 80 per cent of this profit was distributed on Christmas Day. Small as this bonus was—in the good years it amounted to no more than a month's pay, or a month's earnings—it was greatly appreciated, and the goodwill and willing co-operation it ensured, enabled me to handle a million tons of goods a year for twenty-one years without one single unpleasant incident, and without one single day's stoppage of work.